ON THE *GLAUBENSLEHRE*

AMERICAN ACADEMY OF RELIGION
TEXTS AND TRANSLATIONS SERIES

Edited by
James A. Massey

Number 3
ON THE *GLAUBENSLEHRE*
Friedrich D. E. Schleiermacher
Translated by James Duke and Francis Fiorenza

FRIEDRICH D. E. SCHLEIERMACHER

ON THE *GLAUBENSLEHRE*
TWO LETTERS TO DR. LÜCKE

Translated by James Duke and Francis Fiorenza

SCHOLARS PRESS

Distributed by
Scholars Press
101 Salem Street
Chico, CA 95926

ON THE *GLAUBENSLEHRE*
TWO LETTERS TO DR. LÜCKE

Friedrich D. E. Schleiermacher
Translated by James Duke and Francis Fiorenza

Library of Congress Cataloging in Publication Data

Schleiermacher, Friedrich Ernst Daniel, 1768–1834
   On the Glaubenslehre.

   (Texts and translations series — American Academy of
Religion ; no. 3)
   Translation of Schleiermachers Sendschreiben über seine
Glaubenslehre an Lücke.
   Includes bibliographical references and indexes.
   1. Schleiermacher, Friedrich Ernst Daniel, 1768–1834. Der
christliche glaube. 2. Theology, Doctrinal. I. Lücke, Friedrich,
1791–1855. II. Title. III. Series: American Academy of
Religion. Texts and translations series — American Academy of
Religion ; no. 3.
BT75.S587S3413   230'.044   80-20717
ISBN 0-89130-419-3
ISBN 0-89130-420-7 (pbk.)

Printed in the United States of America
1 2 3 4 5
Edwards Brothers, Inc.
Ann Arbor, Michigan 48106

TABLE OF CONTENTS

	PAGE
ABBREVIATIONS	ix
TRANSLATORS' INTRODUCTION	1
THE FIRST LETTER	33
THE SECOND LETTER	55
NOTES TO THE TRANSLATORS' INTRODUCTION	91
NOTES TO THE FIRST LETTER	95
NOTES TO THE SECOND LETTER	119
TABLE OF COMPARATIVE PAGINATION	131
INDEX OF NAMES IN THE TEXT	133
INDEX OF NAMES IN THE NOTES	135

This translation of Schleiermacher's *On the Glaubenslehre* originated in the Nineteenth Century Theology Working Group of the American Academy of Religion. An Advisory Committee of that Group is responsible for the selection of projects and the editing of manuscripts. The Advisory Committee consists of:

Francis S. Fiorenza (Catholic University of America)
Van A. Harvey (Stanford University)
Peter C. Hodgson (Vanderbilt University)
Robert P. Scharlemann (University of Iowa)
Jack Verheyden (Claremont School of Theology)
Claude Welch (Graduate Theological Union)

The editor wishes to express his thanks to the Advisory Committee for making this translation available to the Texts and Translations Series.

James A. Massey

ABBREVIATIONS

ASL   Dilthey, Wilhelm, ed. *Aus Schleiermachers Leben, In Briefen.* 4 vols. Berlin: Georg Reimer, 1861-63.

CG   Friedrich Schleiermacher, *Der christliche Glaube nach den Grundsätzen der evangelischen Kirche im Zusammenhange dargestellt.* 2 vols. Berlin: G. Reimer, [1]1821-22; [2]1830-31. A critical edition with appendices and Schleiermacher's own marginal notes, listed as the 7th printing based on the 2d ed., has been prepared by Martin Redeker. 2 vols. Berlin: Walter de Gruyter, 1960.

E.T.   English Translation

FThPh   *Für Theologie und Philosophie: Eine Oppositionsschrift*

JP   *Journal für Prediger*

StGW   *Studien der evangelischen Geistlichkeit Wirtembergs*

SW   *Friedrich Schleiermachers sämmtliche Werke.* 31 vols. divided into 3 pts. Berlin: G. Reimer, 1835-64.

ThStK   *Theologische Studien und Kritiken*

TZTh   *Tübinger Zeitschrift für Theologie*

ZThK   *Zeitschrift für Theologie und Kirche*

THE SIGNIFICANCE OF *ON THE GLAUBENSLEHRE*

On the Glaubenslehre: Two Letters to Dr. Lücke represents
Friedrich Schleiermacher's apologia for his dogmatic theology.
The first edition of *The Christian Faith* had sold out within a
few years after its publication in 1821-22. As early as August
of 1825 the publisher asked Schleiermacher to prepare a new edition,
but other responsibilities kept him from beginning the revision
until 1828. By that time he felt the task to be complicated by
the necessity of responding to the varied appraisals of his work
made by its reviewers. Rather than clutter the new edition with
defenses and refutations, he chose to argue his case in these two
letters written to his friend Friedrich Lücke and published in
Theologische Studien und Kritiken.[1]

The *Letters to Lücke* is a rich resource for understanding
Schleiermacher's theology. It reveals how he viewed the reception
of *The Christian Faith*, and it serves as an introduction to the
differences between its two editions, indicating how seriously
Schleiermacher took his critics as he prepared the revision.[2]
Especially significant is the commentary on *The Christian Faith*
that Schleiermacher provides. Distressed by what he sees as misreadings of his work, he attempts to clarify many of the concepts
and issues central to his thought. At the same time he brings to
light underlying concerns that shape his dogmatics. Sensitive to
the shaking of theological foundations in his day, he expresses
his view of the plight and promise of theology in the modern era,
and he envisions the formation of "an eternal covenant between the
living Christian faith and completely free, independent scientific
inquiry, so that faith does not hinder science and science does
not exclude faith."[3]

The discussions in *The Letters to Lücke* do make certain
special demands upon the reader. As he wrote the work, Schleiermacher could assume that his readers would be familiar with the
first edition of *The Christian Faith* and with its reviews and
reviewers. But the situation today is quite different. The first
edition of the dogmatics is no longer in print, and information
about most of the reviews and reviewers must be gained from
specialized and often hard-to-obtain research materials.

Therefore, in this Introduction it is appropriate to comment
on the relationship between the two editions of *The Christian Faith*,
to relate them to other Schleiermacher texts, and to separate key

1

issues from the tangle of personalities and opinions with which
Schleiermacher contends. Moreover, it is proper to make a preliminary statement on the significance of *The Letters to Lücke*
for Schleiermacher interpretation. We will focus attention on
three dominant themes: Schleiermacher's conception of dogmatics,
his understanding of piety, and his view of the relationship
between theology and philosophy.

I. *Schleiermacher's Conception of Dogmatics*

Schleiermacher was aware that *The Christian Faith* was dogmatic theology in a new key. Standard theological handbooks were
designed either to elaborate biblical and creedal loci or to
renovate the doctrinal tradition by recourse to philosophical
first principles. In contrast, Schleiermacher's point of departure
is the religious self-consciousness shared by Christians in the
church. Theology, he claims, is the product of disciplined and
critical reflection on that corporate experience. To dogmatic
theology falls the special task of exhibiting "the connectedness
of the doctrine prevailing in a Christian community at a certain
time."[4] Thus, he can refer to his own system as the church's
"doctrine of faith" or *Glaubenslehre*.

Readers were to be oriented to this new approach in the
Introduction to the work. The dogmatics proper was to set forth
the actual content of Christian self-understanding. In order to
appraise the system, then, reviewers had to take stock of this
conception of dogmatics, and immediately two interrelated issues
came to the fore: the significance of the Introduction and the
appropriateness of the overall design of the work.

The Introduction to *The Christian Faith*

The conception of dogmatics presented in the Introduction to
The Christian Faith builds upon the description of the theological
task that Schleiermacher had given in his *Brief Outline on the
Study of Theology*, published in 1811. There theology is said to
be a "positive science" that encompasses "the scientific knowledge
and practical instruction" necessary for church leaders, who are
to understand and advance the true concerns of the community of
faith. The range of this knowledge and instruction is broad, as
many fields of study come into play. But this assembly of elements
gains unity because the components relate to a "particular mode
of faith, i.e., a particular way of being conscious of God,"
shared by church members.[5]

Schleiermacher divides theology into three branches. Philosophical theology, in collaboration with the philosophy of religion,
is to identify the essence of Christianity as a distinctive mode
of religious self-consciousness. Historical theology seeks to
compare at every point in history the state of the church in relationship to the essence of the faith. Practical theology is to
suggest "the correct procedures for executing all of the tasks"
incumbent upon church leaders. In this scheme, dogmatics is defined as that branch of historical theology dealing with the public
teaching of the contemporary church.[6]

The expositions of this definition, both in *The Brief Outline*
and in the Introduction to *The Christian Faith*, make it clear that
dogmatic theology is ecclesial, descriptive, and historical. It
is ecclesial in that it is rooted in the Christian religious self-
consciousness and is undertaken in the service of the church. It
is descriptive in that it is to display in a precise and coherent
manner the content of Christian teaching. It is historical in
that it must express that content in a form appropriate to the
situation in which the church finds itself. The theologian must
therefore relate the consciousness of God distinctive to the
Christian community, the stock of inherited statements expressive
of that consciousness, and the patterns of thought current in the
present age.

Schleiermacher's comments about religious language serve to
clarify further the character of dogmatic theology.[7] Religious
self-consciousness, he explains, quite naturally expresses itself
in language. These expressions are at first predominately poetical,
arising more or less spontaneously from heightened religious emotion, and rhetorical, aimed at persuading others to share in the
religious life. In order to understand the full meaning of their
faith, however, Christians begin to reflect upon their experience
and connect it to the totality of their life-relations. From this
reflection emerges a third form of language, the descriptively
didactic.

In dogmatic theology, descriptively-didactic language is
employed at the highest level of intellectual sophistication. Its
usage is marked by conceptual precision, systematic coherence, and
comprehensiveness, and these characteristics set dogmatics apart
from such popular forms of communication as sermons and catechisms.
In addition, the language of dogmatics unites both ecclesiastical
and scientific values; that is, dogmatic propositions must always
refer to their source in religious self-consciousness, and they
must conform to the standards of intelligibility proper to

scientific inquiry.[8]

By the proper combination of these values, dogmatics can
serve the church by eliminating confused thinking about the nature
and meaning of faith and by distinguishing genuinely Christian
teaching from "worldly wisdom."[9] In Schleiermacher's judgment,
traditional church dogmatics, bound to scholastic and philosophical alliances, were incapable of guiding the church in the post-
enlightenment milieu. Only a total reconsideration of Christian
teaching, taking into account both the essence of Christianity
and the current cultural setting, could help the church face the
crises of the present and of the coming future. *The Christian
Faith* was not merely a reformulation of individual doctrines, but
a new model for doing dogmatic theology.

In the first edition, the Introduction moved from the
definition of dogmatics to a series of analyses of the nature of
the religious self-consciousness, the essence of Christianity,
and the relationship between Christianity and other forms of
religious associations. At that point Schleiermacher was prepared to discuss the design of the system itself.[10]

Although irenic in tone, the Introduction occasioned great
controversy. Since the conception of dogmatics was obviously
linked to, if not dictated by, the analyses of the essence of
Christianity, reviewers regarded the Introduction as the foundation for the entire system. But they differed over what kind of
foundation this was. Some saw it as a theoretical foundation for
dogmatics, a product of philosophical speculation, which was
variously termed "pantheistic," "idealistic," or "gnostic." The
treatment of the doctrinal tradition in the body of the work was
taken to be a willful attempt to bring theology into line with
certain dangerous tendencies in modern philosophy. Others saw it
as a non-theoretical foundation. According to this line of interpretation, Schleiermacher's appeals to religious self-consciousness robbed faith of all cognitive content. And since the Introduction failed either to demonstrate or to presuppose any timeless
and universally valid truths of faith, the accounts of individual
doctrines were suspect from the start.

In response to these criticisms, Schleiermacher tries in
The Letters to Lücke to clarify the intent of the Introduction and
its relationship to dogmatics proper. It is wrong, he maintains,
to consider the Introduction "the main subject and core of the work,"
for in fact it was meant to be only "a preliminary orientation
which, strictly speaking, lies outside of the discipline of

dogmatics itself" and is radically different from the rest of
the book.[11]

He concedes that he may have been partly to blame for this
misinterpretation. By beginning with a definition of dogmatics
and then moving on to the complex of analyses, he may have given
the impression that the Introduction itself was an intrinsic part
of the system. In order to correct that problem, he promises that
in the second edition he will attempt to separate the Introduction
more clearly from the dogmatic materials. The propositions in
the Introduction are to be rearranged and, in some cases, rewritten
and grouped under subheadings that indicate the train of thought.

This plan was in fact carried out. The first proposition
in the second edition no longer deals with the nature of dogmatics,
but with the purpose of the Introduction, which is "first, to set
forth the conception of Dogmatics which underlies the work itself;
and secondly, to prepare the reader for the method and arrangement
followed in it."[12] Since the statements on the church, the diver-
sity of religious communions, and the essence of Christianity had
been mistakenly regarded as part of dogmatics itself, these are
now marked out as propositions borrowed from ethics, the philosophy of religion and apologetics, respectively. This new
arrangement underscores that these analyses belong to other fields
of inquiry rather than to dogmatics and that they prepare the way
for the definition of dogmatics itself because "we can only explain what it is when we have become clear as to the conception
of the Christian Church."[13]

With regard to the substance of the charges against him,
Schleiermacher denies that the Introduction lays a foundation for
his dogmatic theology. In doing so, he must respond both to those
who claim he offers a theoretical foundation as well as to those
who claim the foundation is non-theoretical. He tries to assure
the first group of critics that, although the analyses in the
Introduction employ philosophical categories, they are merely
descriptive in nature and serve only to locate Christian piety,
as it actually exists, within the context of religious life.
He disavows any attempt to ground, found, or prove faith itself.[14]

In his judgment--and here he touches on the concern shared by
all his critics--philosophy should not and cannot provide the basis
for religious faith. Religious self-consciousness is presented
both to the theologian and the philosopher as a given for reflection. It prompts intellectualization, but it is not itself produced by intellectual argument. The theologian, then, reflects on
religious experience, and that reflection may make use of

philosophical categories in order to clarify but not to construct
the data of religion.

To those who claim that the Introduction provides a non-
theoretical basis for dogmatics that robs Christianity of its
content, Schleiermacher responds that the religious self-consciousness present in the historic Christianity community provides all
of the proper content for theology. If religious self-consciousness yielded no knowledge, there would indeed be no occasion for
theology at all. In fact, however, it does supply precisely what
is needed, as the dogmatic system itself demonstrates. Content
coming from other sources would not be appropriate for *Christian*
teaching. And the notion that the essence of Christianity rests
in certain "ideas" derived from reason and/or revelation is de-
leterious to the church because it leads to a distinction between
those Christians who properly comprehend the ideas and those whose
conceptions are deficient or imperfect. Given this distinction,
one would have to assume that the latter group has either no faith
at all or one derived from the theologians rather than from personal life. The distinction therefore calls into question the
fundamental equality of all in Christ. It also overlooks the fact
that many truly religious persons may lack philosophical and
speculative abilities, whereas many theologians may lack Christian
piety, despite their conceptual mastery of religious ideas.
Schleiermacher does not think it wise, then, to expect theology to
provide a basis for Christianity, and he insists that the Introduction to *The Christian Faith* makes no attempt to do so.[15]

The Design of *The Christian Faith*

At the conclusion of the Introduction, Schleiermacher discusses the range of materials to be covered in dogmatics as well
as the design to be followed in handling these materials. He carefully circumscribes the range of materials within limits set by
his understanding of Christian doctrines as expressions of the
religious self-consciousness distinctive to the Christian community.
The final two propositions deal specifically with the organizational scheme of the system, and it was about these especially that
reviewers raised serious questions.[16]

Schleiermacher organizes his system along the lines suggested
by his analyses of the structure of Christian religious self-consciousness.[17] This structure has two elements. There is a consciousness of God, rooted in a feeling of absolute dependence,
which is part of the constitution of human selfhood. There is also
a distinctive modification or determination of that

God-consciousness by a "felt opposition" between an inability on
the part of the self to permit the God-consciousness to predominate
in every moment of life and an ability to do so communicated by
the redeemer, Jesus Christ.

Both elements are always present in Christian experience.
But, since at different times the one or the other has come strongly to the fore, Christian reflection has produced some doctrines
expressing most directly the God-consciousness itself and other
doctrines expressing primarily the felt opposition, or, as
Schleiermacher calls it, the antithesis of sin and grace. Therefore, Schleiermacher chooses to discuss, first, those expressions
of religious self-consciousness "apart from the antithesis" and,
second, those "under" or within the antithesis.

In accordance with this plan, the first division of *The
Christian Faith* treats doctrines expressing the God-consciousness
which, considered in and of itself, is given as part of human
selfhood. These refer to the general relationship between God and
the world and include the so-called metaphysical attributes of
God. Schleiermacher anticipates that readers might take this
discussion to be part of some universal or natural theology rather
than of Christian dogmatics. He concedes that the distinctively
Christian element is in this division "less prominent" and that
many of the statements in it, expressing no more than monotheism
per se, may coincide with beliefs held in non-Christian religions.
Yet he emphasizes that they must be included in Christian dogmatics
because they do in fact arise from the religious self-consciousness
within the Christian church.

The second division of his work deals with doctrines that express the consciousness of sin and grace. Here the distinctively
Christian element is clear. But these doctrines are not unrelated
to the description of the general relationship between God and
the world. Although they introduce material that does not appear
in the first division, they are not simply *addenda*. Rather they
presuppose and complete the discussions in the first division.
God-consciousness and the antithesis of sin and grace are always
in Christianity co-present and interrelated. Together they comprise
the proper range of dogmatics because they encompass Christian
religious experience as a unified whole.

Schleiermacher concludes his account of the design of his work
by discussing dogmatic propositions themselves.[18] These are of
three types: descriptions of human states, conceptions of divine
attributes and modes of action, and statements about the constitution of the world. Christianity has of course produced

propositions of all three types, but Schleiermacher designates
the first as the "fundamental dogmatic form" because it expresses
inner religious experience alone. Since the other two could have
arisen from such non-religious sources as metaphysics and natural
science, they are permitted in dogmatic theology only insofar as
they can be shown to have developed from the first form, that is,
from religious experience. Strictly speaking, dogmatics could
omit them entirely because they add no new content to that given
in religious experience itself. But due to their prominence in
the doctrinal tradition, in the life of the church, and in contemporary debates about religion, Schleiermacher decides that they
must be included in his work. Only in this way can his dogmatics
serve to guide the church in coming to a proper understanding of
the content they express. In every case, then, the task will be
to show their essential connection to descriptions of religious
self-consciousness.

Reviewers objected to both Schleiermacher's organizational
schema and his account of dogmatic propositions. His decision
to begin with the general relationship between God and the world
was cited as further evidence of his resolve to subject Christianity to general philosophical principles. His rationale for including discussions of all three types of dogmatic propositions was
found unacceptable. Since these propositions include discussions
of the historical Jesus and many topics long regarded as essential
to Christianity, reviewers came to believe the Schleiermacher was
willing to jettison the very heart of the faith. His refusal to
do so was seen by some as an attempt to give the appearance of
orthodoxy and by others as a failure to be critical enough of
orthodox theology.

In response to questions about the design of his dogmatics,
Schleiermacher sets forth in *The Letters to Lücke* his reasons for
organizing the work as he did.[19] He admits that he had considered
reversing the two major divisions of the work. If he had begun
with doctrines that express the religious self-consciousness distinctive to Christianity, readers would understand that his aim
was to describe Christian experience and that every doctrine referred back to the center of faith. It would then be evident that
a concern for religion no less than for science, i.e., philosophy,
guided the construction. Moreover, the discussion of the general
relationship between God and the world would take on its proper
meaning and tone when placed in the context of his Christology,
ecclesiology, and exposition of divine love and wisdom.[20]

Nonetheless, Schleiermacher chose not to reorganize his work.
The system, he decided, should conclude with the crucial section
dealing with the fullness and particularity of Christian awareness.
Otherwise the ending of the book would be "anticlimactic." Furthermore, if the section on sin and grace were to come first, it
would have to borrow upon materials from the section on God and
the world, leaving that section so abstract and schematic that it
could no longer serve the purpose of clarifying many difficult
issues present there.

Schleiermacher explains why it is possible even to consider
such a reordering of the system.[21] Dogmatic systematization is a
peculiar sort. Since the unity of the whole is vested in religious
self-consciousness, it does not matter where one begins the discussion. Indeed, the possibility of such a revision indicate that
dogmatics stays within its proper sphere and seeks only to be a
skillful arrangement of elements that are in experience co-present
and intertwined.

Schleiermacher therefore limits his changes in the second edition to sharpening the language of the discussion. The two divisions are now referred to as doctrines "presupposed by the antithesis of sin and grace" and those "determined by the antithesis."[22]
These headings, as well as the expositions, emphasize more strongly
the connectedness of the two elements in religious self-consciousness.

With respect to criticisms of his account of dogmatic propositions, Schleiermacher only reaffirms in *The Letters to Lücke* his
original position. He maintains that *all* of the essential content
of theology is to be found in propositions of the first type.
There is no reason to fear, then, that the historical Jesus, as
the fundament of faith, or any other essential element would be
omitted by a dogmatics containing only "descriptions of human
states of mind." At present, however, he is convinced that dogmatics can meet the needs of the church only be taking into consideration the full range of Christian teaching, which includes doctrines about divine attributes and the constitution of the world.

The proper treatment of those doctrines, however, requires a
dialectical polemic, which begins with current teaching and then
subjects it to examination.[23] The dogmatician must show at every
point that the religious self-consciousness is original and indispensable. Dogmatic propositions must express this religious self-
consciousness in such a way that they harmonize with one another
as well as with other provinces of human knowledge.

In evaluating Schleiermacher's conception of dogmatics, the
reviewers were forced to grapple with his understanding of the relationship between theology and philosophy. In the first edition
of *The Christian Faith* Schleiermacher had stated, rather indefinite-
ly, that dogmatics is "in a certain sense and measure dependent
upon philosophy." In the second edition he explains that his
dependence concerns the "form" rather than the content of dogmatic
propositions.[24]

Obviously one can ask whether there can be such a strict
separation between form and content, just as one can ask whether
religious self-consciousness can be granted primacy over both
theology and philosophy. Indeed, the second is the prior question,
which turns on Schleiermacher's claim that the religious self-
consciousness carries with it an "immediate existential relationship" with God.[25] It is necessary to discuss, then, Schleiermacher's account of religious self-consciousness and then his conception of the relationship between philosophy and theology.

II. *The Religious Self-Consciousness or Piety*

Central to Schleiermacher's dogmatics is his understanding of
religious self-consciousness or, as he calls it, piety. This
account, however, moves through several complex stages. Piety is
first said to have its locus in feeling. Feeling is then specified
as an immediate self-consciousness of absolute dependence. Finally,
immediate self-consciousness is explained to mean "that we feel
ourselves absolutely dependent upon God."[26] In Schleiermacher's
opinion, many of his critics failed to distinguish these moments
and for this reason misinterpreted his position. In *The Letters
to Lücke*, he tries to correct their misreadings.

Reviewers raised entire sets of issues that strike at the
very heart of Schleiermacher's definition of piety. One set concerned the specification of piety as feeling. This specification,
reviewers complained, robs Christianity of its cognitive content.
Since feeling is subjective, transitory, even unconscious, confused,
and mysterious, it cannot be the core of the Christian religion.
In order to preserve the content of the faith, piety must be
based in knowledge.

A second set of objections was directed to the claim that piety
is a feeling of absolute dependence. Does not absolute dependence
conflict with mature personal autonomy? Does it not make piety
immature, childish, and even subhuman? Would it not undermine
the freedom and responsibility upon which all morality is based?

A third set of criticisms related to the correlation between the feeling of absolute dependence and consciousness of God. Some critics argued that this correlation served to divinize the human being because the self could not equate its absolute dependence and consciousness of God unless it were experiencing itself as part of the divine nature. Other critics claimed that, since humans experience a total dependence on nature, this correlation leads inevitably to pantheism. Given these differing interpretations, as well as Schleiermacher's repudiation of them both, what is the precise nature between feeling and knowledge of God?

Schleiermacher takes care to respond to all three sets of issues both in *The Letters to Lücke* and in his revisions of *The Christian Faith*. In each case he appeals to his analysis of the nature of piety, and for this reason each of the moments in that analysis deserves some consideration.

Piety

The very choice of the term piety to designate the essence of religion requires some explanation. Although Schleiermacher refers to his dogmatics as the *Glaubenslehre* or doctrine of faith, it is piety (*Frömmigkeit*) rather than faith that assumes the central significance in his work. This choice is somewhat surprising when one considers that in Schleiermacher's time the word "piety" was often taken to have a negative connotation. In *Religion within the Limits of Reason Alone*, for example, Kant regards piety as a surrogate of virtue. It refers to a passive attitude to a godliness that comes from above and so is not autonomous.[27] Schleiermacher is not unfamiliar with this pejorative and, in his judgment, incorrect, usage of the word.[28] Yet he prefers to restore the word to its "proper" meaning rather than to discard it.

The significance of his decision is to be seen in light of the meaning of the terms "piety" and "faith" (*Glaube*) within the dogmatic tradition. First, the word "faith" emerged from discussions about the relations of *notitia, assensus*, and *fiducia*. In these the content or object of faith (*fides quae creditur*) was given primary emphasis and the manner or power of faith (*fides quā creditur*) was relegated to secondary consideration. Secondly, the word "pious" (*fromm*) harkened back to the reformation. The Zurich Bible used the word to translate *justificatus*. Pietism of course brought the term once again into prominence, and with its emphasis upon rebirth and sanctification, the terms piety (*Frömmigkeit*) and divine salvation (*Gottseligkeit*) served to accent these aspects

of Christianity. Thus, when Schleiermacher refers to piety, the
Christian pious self-consciousness, and the Christian pious affections, he is interpreting the "doctrine of faith" more in the
sense of a determination of Christian life than in the sense of
faith as intellectual assent.[29]

Feeling

According to Schleiermacher, piety is located in feeling.
But in everyday usage the term "feeling" is especially ambivalent,
and this ambivalence troubled Schleiermacher's critics. Feeling
may refer to sensations coming from the external world or to states
of awareness induced internally within consciousness. Indeed, as
some critics were quick to point out, one can speak even of unconscious feelings. What is crucial, claimed the critics, is not
feeling but the object that produces this feeling. This object
gives Christianity its specific content.

Schleiermacher's own understanding of feeling was developed
over a long course of time, as is evident from his treatment of the
topic in his lectures on psychology and ethics as well as in the
Dialektik and *The Christian Faith*.[30] These accounts are not
totally uniform, but manifest accents that are at times quite
varied, especially with regard to the relation between feeling and
immediate self-consciousness.

Despite the variations, however, there are certain continui-
ties. First, although Schleiermacher starts out from the tripartite
division of selfhood (feeling, knowing, and willing) common to the
psychology of his day, he is not seeking to perpetuate faculty
psychology. To the contrary, he cuts across the tripartite scheme
by means of a twofold division of spontaneous and receptive activities. Life is a constant oscillation between an "abiding in self"
and a "passing beyond self." It is true that there is a development
of his thought on this matter, too. In the *Psychologie*, feeling is
understood as the "receptive *activity* of consciousness"; in *The
Christian Faith*, the pure passivity and internality of feeling
are stressed.[31] In any case, the term "feeling" has a quite precise, even technical, meaning for Schleiermacher.

Second, Schleiermacher constantly underscores the foundational
role of feeling in relation to the activities of consciousness.
This role is granted to feeling in the *Psychologie* as well as
The Christian Faith, although the latter work emphasizes it even
more. Feeling is a structure of consciousness in which the self
is aware of its unified existence throughout the changing acts of
consciousness in thinking and willing. This awareness is interior,

constant, and cohesive, whereas thinking and willing relate to
changing objects of thought and volitional projects.

Third, although Schleiermacher admits that in ordinary speech
a "feeling" may be said to be internally or externally induced,
and even unconscious, he insists that he is not using the word in
such a broad sense.[32] He relates feeling, instead, to immediate
self-consciousness, and he is concerned to emphasize that relationship in *The Christian Faith*. In the first edition he had introduced
this topic by stating simply: "Piety is in itself neither a knowing
nor a doing, but an inclination and a specification of feeling."
The revision in the second edition, however, is more precise:
"The piety which forms the basis of all ecclesiastical communions
is, considered in itself, neither a Knowing nor a Doing, but a modification of Feeling, or of immediate self-consciousness."[33]
What, then, is immediate self-consciousness?

Immediate Self-Consciousness

In *The Christian Faith*, Schleiermacher describes piety by
reference to the structures constitutive of selfhood. The life of
the self is constituted by two structures or levels of self-
consciousness. At one level, the sensible self-consciousness, there
is a constant interchange of thinking and willing as the subject
deals with the various objects of awareness--perceptions, ideas,
fantasies, and the like. At the other level, that of immediate
self-consciousness, there is a structure that grounds and unifies
the various acts of thinking and willing. This structure is "the
mediating link" between moments in which knowing predominates and
those in which doing predominates, and as such it can be termed
the essence of the subject itself.[34]

It is important to distinguish these two structures because
feeling is related to immediate self-consciousness. There are of
course moments when a consciousness of self is objective.[35]
Consciousness can reflect upon itself and become aware of itself
as one object among others. This self-consciousness, however, is
reflective, not immediate. Such reflection already presupposes
that there is a structure of self-consciousness that makes possible
the reflective act. Thus, Schleiermacher emphasizes that he is
concerned with *immediate* self-consciousness, the direct presence
of total undivided existence.

On the basis of this description of immediate self-consciousness, one can understand better the complex relation between feeling
and self-consciousness. The reflective or mediated self-consciousness in which one perceives oneself as an object is not a feeling.

Feeling refers rather to the immediate self-consciousness in which
the self is "with itself" and closer to itself than in acts of
reflection. This awareness is not unconscious nor an unconscious-
ness, but an immediate awareness of the determination of the self.

The lived immediacy of this awareness may be illustrated by
an example. In the moment of shame, one does not distinguish
between the self and the shame, but one is a shamed self. As soon
as one reflects on the experience, one can distinguish between
the shame and the self as two distinct things. The shame and the
self are no longer immediate, but objectified through reflection.

This conception of immediate self-consciousness helps explain
the differentiation of feeling from knowing and doing. Immediate
self-consciousness is both distinct and yet related to knowing
and doing. Immediate self-consciousness mediates between the
individual acts of consciousness, accompanying them and unifying
them in a presence of the totality of the self.

Yet, according to Schleiermacher, immediate self-consciousness
is by no means just an "accompaniment," as can be confirmed by two
types of experience available to everyone.[36] The first occurs
in moments when thinking and willing withdraw, leaving the self-
consciousness as such to predominate. The second occurs when the
same mode of self-consciousness persists throughout changing acts
of thinking and willing.

Schleiermacher emphasizes, then, both aspects of immediate
self-consciousness. It is related to and yet distinct from the
various acts of thinking and willing. Here the unity of human
existence is manifest to itself.

The Feeling of Absolute Dependence

In piety, immediate self-consciousness is modified in such a
way that the unity of the self is made present to the self as
"absolutely dependent." In order to explicate this feeling,
Schleiermacher refers again to an analysis of life experiences.
Thinking, willing, and feeling are compared in terms of the antithesis between receptivity and spontaneity or dependence and freedom. In thinking and willing, consciousness is characterized by
an awareness of partial freedom and partial dependence vis-à-vis
its objects. Consciousness relates to its objects by receiving an
influence from them and acting upon them in cognition and volition.
Taken as a whole, these relations may be called the realm of
reciprocity, and they constitute the sensible self-consciousness
of the self. Since the realm of reciprocity encompasses all human
relations with nature, other selves, and with the world as a

whole, it is in actuality the sum of finite relations with the
finite world.

Immediate self-consciousness, however, is not characterized
by a reciprocity of receptivity and activity on the part of the
self, but by sheer receptivity. The unity of the self is experienced as irreducibly given, produced neither by the self nor by
any object susceptible to a counter-influence from the self.
This "modification" or mode of determination of immediate self-
consciousness Schleiermacher calls "the feeling of absolute
dependence." He also refers to it as the "higher self-consciousness," which encompasses--founds, unified, and accompanies--the
varied determinations of the sensible self-consciousness.

No less controversial than Schleiermacher's definition of
piety as feeling was his specification of that feeling as absolute
dependence. Numerous critics objected that his account of religious
feeling eliminated human freedom, reduced piety to a subhuman
level, and implied that the development of the individual human
personality was sinful. Ths most famous criticism was perhaps
that made by Hegel in his "Foreword to Hinrich's *Religionsphilosophie*":

> Should feeling constitute the basic determination of
> human nature, then humans are equated with animals,
> for feeling is what is specific to animals. It con-
> stitutes their essence and they live according to
> feeling. If religion in humans is based on a feeling,
> then such a feeling has correctly no further speci-
> fication than to be the *feeling of its dependence*.
> Consequently, a dog would be the best Christian, since
> a dog is most strongly characterized by this feeling
> and lives primarily in this feeling. Moreover, then,
> the dog also has the feeling of redemption if his
> hunger is satisfied through a bone. The spirit has
> in religion, however, its liberation and the feeling
> of its divine freedom, and only the free spirit
> possesses religion and can possess religion.[37]

Schleiermacher was not unaware that Hegel and others had
lodged such objections against him.[38] But he believed them to be
without foundation. Indeed, in *The Letters to Lücke* he expresses
dismay over this interpretation of feeling. He maintains that, far
from denying human freedom, he affirms it. And, in fact, an examination of his arguments in *The Christian Faith* shows that Schleiermacher rejects an either-or between human freedom and absolute
dependence.[39]

Schleiermacher first seeks to demonstrate that absolute dependence and human freedom are compatible. But it is clearly
finite freedom of which he speaks. Within the realm of finitude,
the individual has the capacity to act and to be acted upon.
Every moment of thinking and willing is marked by partial freedom

and partial dependence. The self-consciousness that unifies these
moments, however, is present to itself as a given,
and thus absolutely dependent. As the "foundation" or "mediating
link" between relations of partial (finite) freedom and dependence,
feeling coexists with these experiences.

The account of absolute dependence in the first edition of
The Christian Faith had prompted so much criticism that Schleiermacher decided to revise it extensively for the second edition.
In the first edition Schleiermacher had tried to explain absolute
dependence by the use of finite analogies. Citing such natural
relations of dependence as those of children upon parents and
citizens upon their country, he spoke of a gradation of dependencies
of which the highest was the feeling of absolute dependence.
In the second edition, however, the notion of gradations was eliminated so that the contrast between experiences of partial freedom
and partial dependence and those of absolute dependence comes more
clearly into view.[40] Absolute dependence is shown to have a
different character than finite dependencies because it is marked
by the absence of any counter-influence on the part of the subject.

This contrast is further developed by means of an analysis of
the interrelations between experiences of freedom and dependence.
In Schleiermacher's judgment, such an analysis demonstrates that
there is no experience of absolute freedom and that the feeling of
absolute dependence is on a level quite distinct from our experiences of partial freedom and partial dependence.

The feeling of freedom is that of activity outwardly directed
toward some object. The object, however, must somehow be given
to consciousness. If it comes from the external world, then of
course the self experiences not only freedom, **but** also a receptivity,
a resistance or limit to freedom. And even if the source of the
object is only an inward movement or activity, the awareness of
freedom is bound up with a state of stimulated receptivity and
occurs within the temporal nexus of relations between the self and
its objects. Even taking the totality of our free inward movements
as a whole, it is necessary to acknowledge that humans do not experience themselves as creators of objects, temporality, or their
own existence. In short, "our whole existence does not present itself to our consciousness as having proceeded from our own spontaneous activity."[41]

The same argument is then used to clarify the nature of absolute dependence. It does not relate to any given object, moment
of time, or segment of activity because in these cases some
counter-influence or relative freedom is possible.

> But the self-consciousness which accompanies all
> our activity, and therefore, since that is never
> zero, accompanies our whole existence, and nega-
> tives absolute freedom, is itself precisely a
> consciousness of absolute dependence; for it is
> the consciousness that the whole of our spontan-
> eous activity comes from a source outside of us
> in just the same sense in which anything towards
> which we should have a feeling of absolute freedom
> must have proceed entirely from ourselves. But
> without any feeling of freedom, a feeling of
> absolute dependence would not be possible.[42]

Although Schleiermacher mentions no names in this passage, it
is clear that he is arguing against idealists such as Fichte, who
find the self-positing ego to be the ultimate foundation for all
that is. And it is quite possible that Schleiermacher also has
in mind to what he considers to be Hegel's view of freedom.

In any event, Schleiermacher, at least, is confident that
he preserves and protects human freedom. The feeling of absolute
dependence is not a servile state, but one that makes possible
and accompanies free interactions with the finite world.

Absolute Dependence as a Consciousness
of Relationship to God

Schleiermacher's analysis of piety culminates in the claim
that the feeling of absolute dependence is a consciousness of
relationship to God. Many reviewers found this equation problematic, although on different grounds. Schleiermacher was challenged
on three fronts.

One question was whether Schleiermacher's account of piety
was pantheistic. According to his critics, if feeling is an awareness of the totality of human existence and its relations with
all things, then the connection between feeling and God-consciousness must mean that the word "God" refers to the system of nature
as a whole. As our discussion of feeling demonstrated, Schleiermacher made every effort to put this complaint to rest, for
neither an awareness of any part of the universe nor that of the
universe as a whole can properly be called *absolute* dependence.

It is also to be noted that in the second edition of *The
Christian Faith* Schleiermacher adds a passage emphasizing that
pantheism does arise from direct reflection on piety, but from
some sort of independent philosophical or speculative intellectualization. Thus, it cannot have any role to play in Christian
dogmatics.[43]

The passage in *The Christian Faith* is in harmony with the
comments about pantheism that Schleiermacher makes in

The Letters to Lücke. He assumes that pantheism is a philosophical
position advocated by a number of well-known thinkers. But he
denies that his dogmatics has been influenced by any philosophy,
much less by pantheism, and he tries to show that those critics
who have accused him of pantheism are unable to provide any solid
evidence for their accusation.

A second question asked by some of Schleiermacher's critics
was whether the connection between the human feeling of absolute
dependence and God-consciousness did not identify human subjectivity
as God. If in feeling the unity of the self is inseparable from a
consciousness of God, then Schleiermacher is promoting a philosophy of identity that glorifies or even deifies the human self.
Here again Schleiermacher's account of feeling is intended to
guard against this conclusion because it implies a feeling of absolute freedom or self-creation rather than absolute dependence.
In *The Letters to Lücke*, he tries to counter this view in another
way. His account of self-consciousness, he reminds his readers,
spoke of God-consciousness, world-consciousness, and a consciousness of self.[44] In no case should human awareness of these "objects
of consciousness" be considered their sole reality. Consciousness
of world is not the world itself. Likewise, God-consciousness
and self-consciousness are not God and the self in and of themselves. In short, Schleiermacher wants to distinguish between
consciousness and its determinants. Of course humans can speak
of these determinants only because as they are related to the
structures of human awareness. But these structures are such that
they provide a basis for distinguishing between consciousness and
that of which humans are conscious.

This argument does point out that Schleiermacher does not
identify feeling with God, but, taken in isolation, it is somewhat
misleading because it implies that "God" is an object of consciousness like any other object. This is not, in fact, Schleiermacher's
view of the matter. In order to clarify that view, it is necessary
to consider the third question that Schleiermacher's critics
posed: whether Schleiermacher makes consciousness of God secondary
and derivative to the feeling of absolute dependence.

This issue strikes at the heart of Schleiermacher's understand-
ind of piety, and, in a sense, it takes precedence over the other
two questions. If Schleiermacher is maintaining that there is
first a feeling of absolute dependence and only secondly an interpretation of that feeling as a consciousness of God, he leaves open
the possibility that the interpretation is mistaken. Since the
feeling precedes the identification of that which has determined it,

rival interpretations are certain to emerge. With only Schleiermacher's analysis of feeling to go on, reviewers might well take
his comments about the "unity of the self" and/or "the totality
of the self in relationship to the whole world-order" as the meaning of the word "God."

Schleiermacher had good reason, then, to be concerned about
the precise connection between feeling and God-consciousness. In
The Letters to Lücke he makes a twofold affirmation.[45] He emphasizes the radical immediacy of the feeling of absolute dependence.
The feeling itself is said to be the original expression of an
"immediate existential relationship." He also disavows the suggestion of any prior conditioning of piety by any knowledge or philosophical conception of God. These two affirmations are two sides
of the same coin, since the rejection of prior conditioning is at
the same time the affirmation of immediacy of feeling.

Schleiermacher's revisions of *The Christian Faith* also reflect
his concern for clarity about the connection between feeling and
God-consciousness. The proposition in the first edition had concluded by saying that "we are conscious of ourselves as absolutely
dependent, i.e., that we feel ourselves as absolutely dependent
upon God." In the second edition the proposition is altered to
read: "the self-identical essence of piety: the consciousness of
being absolutely dependent, or, which is the same thing, of being
in relation with God."[46] The transcendental limit of human experience is here more precisely observed. Feeling is not itself God;
nor does it relate to God as an independent "object." Rather,
feeling signifies a *relation* to God.

The exposition also undergoes significant change. In a
Postscript to §9.3 in the first edition, Schleiermacher begins with
a question: "What is earlier, the concept of God or the feeling
of God contained in the pious affections? It is not the proper
place to decide this question here." He then explains that it is
not necessary to presuppose a concept of God derived from somewhere
else because, even if the concept of God were not yet in existence,
reflection on pious feeling would give arise to the thought of the
highest being.[47]

In contrast, the second edition introduces the notion of the
"whence" of our receptive and active existence, which is implied
in religious feeling. Neither the self nor the world, then, but
the "whence" of existence is designated by the word "God."
Schleiermacher then adds:

> in the next place we have to note that our propo-
> sition is intended to oppose the view that this
> feeling of dependence is itself conditioned by some
> previous knowledge of God. And this may indeed be
> the more necessary since many people claim to be in
> the sure possession of a concept of God, altogether
> a matter of conception and original, i.e., indepen-
> dent of feeling; and in the strength of this
> higher self-consciousness, which indeed may come
> pretty near to being a feeling of absolute freedom,
> they put far from them, as something almost infra-
> human, that very feeling which for us is the basic
> type of all piety.[48]

Throughout this section, Schleiermacher is obviously seeking
to respond to the criticisms raised by Hegel and others. Nevertheless, he proceeds very cautiously: "Now our proposition is in no
wise intended to dispute the existence of such an original knowledge, but simply to set it aside as something with which, in a
system of Christian doctrine, we could never have any concern, because plainly enough it itself has nothing to do directly with
piety."[49] Schleiermacher then sums up his argument as follows:

> If, however, word and idea are always originally
> one, and the term "God" therefore presupposes an
> idea, then we shall simply say that this idea,
> which is nothing more than the expression of
> absolute dependence, is the most direct reflection
> upon it and the most original idea with which we
> are here concerned, and is quite independent of
> that original knowledge (properly so called),
> and is conditioned only by our feeling of abso-
> lute dependence. So that in the first instance
> God signified for us simply that which is the
> co-determinant in this feeling and to which we
> trace our being in such a state; and any further
> of the idea must be evolved out of this funda-
> mental import assigned to it.[50]

In short, Schleiermacher does not need to decide whether there is
an original knowledge of God because he is concerned not with acts
of cognition apart from piety but with piety itself, which is the
original and underived basis for theological reflection.

It should be clear that an analysis of Schleiermacher's
statements about piety in *The Letters to Lücke* and the revisions
of *The Christian Faith* aids interpreters by clarifying Schleiermacher's intentions and locating where the real issues lie.
Schleiermacher wants to trace the idea of "God" to the religious
self-consciousness alone, and there is no doubt that he wants to
avoid both pantheism and the divinization of subjectivity. He
seeks to demonstrate that there *is* a co-determinant implied or
co-posited in the feeling of absolute dependence and that that co-
determinant is transcendent in the sense that it is distinguishable
from the world and the self.

These clarifications, however, bring into focus the crucial issue. The argument in the second edition concludes with the statement that God-consciousness is present in the self-consciousness in such a way that the two cannot be separated from each other. "The feeling of absolute dependence becomes a clear self-consciousness only as this idea of God comes simultaneously into being."[51] But how can this claim be squared with Schleiermacher's emphasis on immediacy? Granted that the idea of God is "the most direct reflection" on the feeling of absolute dependence, it none-the less arises from reflection, and therefore is not immediate. And, insofar as feeling is immediate, it is not yet a clear self-consciousness that carries with it a consciousness of God. This ambiguity in Schleiermacher's position did not escape the attention of his critics, and at this point the task of criticism can be taken up and pursued again.

However this key issue is finally decided, it is clear that Schleiermacher has proposed for theology a quite specific approach to the question of knowledge of God. He has also delimited the sphere of dogmatics to that encompassed by religious self-consciousness. Thus, his conception of dogmatics is intimately related to his understanding of piety. He does not foreclose the possibility, however, that philosophy may have much to say about "God." In what respects, then, if any, are philosophy and theology related?

III. Philosophy and Theology

The debates over Schleiermacher's conception of dogmatics and his understanding of piety have repeatedly touched upon matters linked to the relationship between philosophy and theology. In *The Letters to Lücke*, Schleiermacher notes that his various "friends" have urged him to be more explicit about "the relationship between religion and philosophy (as one put it), or between dogmatics and philosophy (as another suggests), or between the higher self-consciousness . . . and the original idea of God . . . (as a third states it)."[52]

As these variations suggest, it is difficult even to formulate the problematic with precision. Since the intention here is limited to the clarification of some of the elements involved in this topic, the choice of the heading "philosophy and theology" is meant only to open up a broad range of concerns. After a few preliminary remarks on the topic itself, attention will focus on questions raised, first, about Schleiermacher's doctrine of God, and, second, about his Christology.

General Considerations

From the beginning, critics of Schleiermacher have disagreed about the role of philosophy in his work. According to one line of interpretation, his dogmatic theology is too dependent upon philosophy or is nothing but a philosophy. Viewed from this perspective, Schleiermacher is seen as a gnostic, a spinozist, a pantheist, or an idealist. The Introduction to *The Christian Faith* is read as a philosophical foundation for dogmatics.

This line of criticism can be traced from Schleiermacher's contemporaries through Ritschlianism and then to its culmination in dialectical theology.[53] Much scholarly attention has been directed toward discerning the influence that Schleiermacher's philosophical contemporaries exerted upon the development of his thought, and many of his key concepts, e.g., his analysis of self-consciousness and his account of religious feeling, have been scrutinized in light of his *Dialektik*.

On the other hand, some critics have argued that Schleiermacher fails adequately to consider and reckon with the philosophical implicationsof his own position. By founding theology in piety, which is independent of philosophical conceptuality, Schleiermacher refuses to acknowledge that the theologian is obliged to engage in philosophical argumentation. Among his contemporaries, Heinrich Schmid, for example, maintained that Schleiermacher's approach fails to meet the standards of critical scientific rationality.[54] And later scholars such as Ernst Troeltsch, Karl Albrecht Bernoulli, and Hermann Süskind agree that Schleiermacher's theological method is not properly "scientific."[55] Even his philosophical theology is dogmatic and ecclesial because it does not raise the critical question about the truth of Christian beliefs.

One is tempted to ask: will the real Schleiermacher stand up? It is by no means easy to predict where he would stand. In *The Letters to Lücke*, Schleiermacher does attempt to shed light on his understanding of the issue by making explicit the basic assumption of his work. Even here, however, he is rather tantalizing. He denies that an explicit account of the relations between theology and philosophy should be included in his dogmatics itself. Since the religious self-consciousness relates to philosophy in the same way that it relates to every other sphere of human activity, there is no cause to single out this relationship for special discussion. As for the relationship between dogmatics and philosophy, he prefers "to speak of it as little as possible."[56]

Despite these disclaimers, there emerges in *The Letters to Lücke* a twofold claim. First, the dogmatician should not philosophize at all in dogmatics. Schleiermacher insists that he did not do so in *The Christian Faith*, which is a presentation of church teaching independent of every philosophical system. Since piety is an immediate existential relation, the explication of its content in dogmatics is independent from philosophy. Second, Schleiermacher maintains that there can be no contradiction between philosophy and theology. Each goes its own way, but, if rightly pursued, the two will not come into conflict. How, then, does Schleiermacher relate the two?

In order to understand Schleiermacher's position, it is helpful to distinguish between the horizon of an author's self-understanding and that of those trying to understand the author. In the first case certain questions come to the fore: What did Schleiermacher mean when he referred to philosophy and theology? What did he see to be the relationship between his *Dialektik* and *The Christian Faith*? How did he attempt in these two works, as well as in his *Brief Outline On the Study of Theology*, to be faithful to the principles expressed in *The Letters to Lücke*?

The second problematic raises a different set of questions. In order to understand Schleiermacher "better than he understood himself," inquirers may consider whether he is to be interpreted in a way that he himself was not fully aware of. Viewed in the context of post-enlightenment romanticism and idealism, does he appear more dependent upon the philosophical categories and the spirit of his time than he realized? Do not his similiarities, and even his differences, with his contemporaries indicate greater dependence on their work than he could recognize or admit?

This distinction of horizons does not magically simplify the question of the relationship between philosophy and theology in Schleiermacher. In some ways it complicates the matter. And, of course, interpretations and evaluations must ultimately involve both considerations. The distinction does make it appropriate, however, to limit the discussion here to an attempt to grasp Schleiermacher's self-understanding and thereby to gain clarity about the problematic itself. Thus, when Schleiermacher insists that his dogmatics is totally independent of philosophy, he should not be taken in the naive sense that he refuses to recognize the presence of any philosophical categories in his work. Rather, he is indicating that he operates with very specific definitions of philosophy and theology.

And, in *The Letters to Lücke*, Schleiermacher does deal with
his understanding of philosophy and theology in very direct terms.[57]
His point is that, if the term philosophy is taken to mean, as
it customarily is, the particular position or system advanced by
a philosopher, say Spinoza, Leibnitz, Kant, Fichte, or Schelling,
then dogmatics can and should be independent. Since dogmatics
arises from Christian piety, the dogmatician will not be beholden
to the philosophers at all. Christian doctrine is neither based
on nor accountable to any given philosophical stance.

Schleiermacher does admit that philosophy impinges on the
formulation of doctrine. But it does so only in two specific and
restricted respects.[58] First, the theologian may choose to employ
categories that are found in philosophical works. But in such
cases the term loses its original meaning and acquires new significance within its distinctively theological context. Secondly,
the formulation of doctrines must seek to meet the standards of
intelligibility and consistency governing rational discourse.
These canons are indeed "philosophical," but they have to do with
the "art of thinking" itself and entail no specific philosophical
allegiance.

With this discussion in mind, it is possible to return again
to the question of how Schleiermacher actually relates philosophy
and theology in his work. It may be suggested that Schleiermacher
understands both theology and philosophy to be reflections on
human experience. They are complementary functions rooted in the
same human spirit. But there is no preordained and necessary
connection between any given philosophical position and the dogmatic exposition of the content of Christian piety.

These preliminary considerations, however, do not serve to
end questions about the influence, if any, that philosophy held
over Schleiermacher's theology. The issue was of special impor-
tance for understanding Schleiermacher's doctrine of God and his
Christology, and his critics raised the same question of each
doctrine: is the determining factor theological or philosophical?

Doctrine of God

So many persons took issue with the doctrine of God presented
in *The Christian Faith* that Schleiermacher was forced to discuss
the relationship between theology and philosophy in *The Letters to
Lücke*. He is especially concerned to refute the charge that his
theology is dependent upon philosophy. For this reason, too, he
attempts in the second edition of *The Christian Faith* to
distinguish between the consciousness of God in piety and the idea

of God discussed in philosophy. In order to understand Schleiermacher's position, it is helpful to refer to his *Dialektik*.

In the *Dialektik* Schleiermacher clarifies his own position
vis-à-vis Kant's critique of rational theology.[59] He is critical
of Kant for positing God solely as a postulate of practical reason,
and as a corrective he argues that God is a necessary postulate of
theoretical reason as well. Yet he agrees with Kant's basic
position insofar as it denies the possibility of a speculative
knowledge of God.

Against the post-Kantian idealists Schleiermacher maintains
that the idea of the divine cannot be known but must always be
presupposed as the identity of thinking and willing with being.
God is not known as are objects of thought and volition, nor is
there knowledge of the identity between knowing and the known.
Rather God is presupposed *as* that identity. This presupposition
is a limit concept, which is designated the "transcendental
ground."[60]

At one crucial point, however, Schleiermacher goes beyond
Kant. Thinking and willing can only presuppose the transcendental
ground. But, as the condition for the possibility of the unity
between thinking and willing, immediate self-consciousness provides
a structure capable of mirroring the transcendental ground. And
Schleiermacher argues that in fact the immediate self-consciousness
is determined by religious feeling in such a way that it serves as
the point of contact between the self and its transcendental
ground.[61]

At this point the difference between philosophy and theology
becomes manifest. In philosophy, the transcendental ground appears
as a presupposition for knowing and willing. In religious feeling,
the immediate self-consciousness is determined by a ground or a
"whence." Philosophy cannot produce this determination of immediate self-consciousness; it can only acknowledge it. Thus,
religious knowledge is not at all derived from philosophical
reflection.

The point may be illustrated by reference to a central but
controversial concept in Kant's moral philosophy, the fact of
pure reason.[62] Kant uses it to refer to the consciousness of the
moral law, which is neither intuited nor deduced, but must be accepted as a fact. The facticity of the moral demand itself becomes the presupposition for a theory accounting for the nature of
the demand. Here Kant places a limit on theoretical reason, although later idealists removed it--Fichte, for example, sought to

deduce consciousness of the moral law from the activity of self-
consciousness.

Schleiermacher's account of religious feeling is similar to
Kant's view of the moral law in that he accepts it as a given and
denies that it can be derived from any more fundamental principle.
Although some persons may regard modifications of the religious
self-consciousness in which immediate self-consciousness is related to the transcendental ground as fictions or deceptions,
Schleiermacher asserts that

> in them there comes to expression the human striving
> to grasp the transcendent. In this there is some-
> thing that neither thinking nor its relation to
> being expresses; these lag behind that [modification
> of immediate self-consciousness]. It can only be
> posited as a fact.[63]

According to Schleiermacher, religious self-consciousness
is an awareness combining affects from the external world in all
its multiplicity and a feeling of the unity that encompasses all
multiplicity. Philosophical reflection attends to this self-
consciousness in terms of its necessity for unifying thinking and
willing. Theological reflection attends to this ground as it is
actually present with and related to elements of the sensible
self-consciousness shaped within a given community of faith.
As a result, philosophy can think the transcendental ground as an
abstract formula; theology thinks it, indeed "anthropomorphizes"
it, as related to the life of piety as a whole. The former has
too little; the latter too much.

Schleiermacher can therefore speak of the relationship between theology and philosophy as that of complementarity and
polarity.[64] The "transcendental ground" or "God" comes into the
purview of both, but in differing ways. From these differing
vantages, discourse about the presupposition of thinking and willing and that about the "whence" of the feeling of absolute dependence move along different lines. In a letter to Jacobi, therefore, Schleiermacher uses the images of an ellipse or oscillation
to express the relationship between the two lines of inquiry.

This interpretation of Schleiermacher's self-understanding
helps explain his responses to his critics in *The Letters to Lücke*.
The modification of self-consciousness in piety is a fact of human
experience that can be neither produced nor eliminated by philosophical analysis. Philosophy and theology both reflect on this
given, but their reflection moves in different directions. For this
reason theological claims are not philosophical, and, vice versa,
philosophical claims are not theological. If reflection is carried
out correctly, however, the two types of claims will not be

contradictory because both will be in accord with the constitution
of immediate self-consciousness. For example, both will affirm
the transcendence of the ground or God from the world. In
philosophy, that transcendence is expressed by the recognition
that the ground is the *presupposition* of thinking and willing. In
theology, that transcendence will be expressed by the use of the
word "God" as the designation of the whence. This transcendence
cannot and should not be transgressed. Both philosophy and theology, each in its own way, speaks of "God" only insofar as the
transcendental ground or the "whence" is accessible to human
reflection.

Obviously one can inquire whether Schleiermacher's account
of the relationship between theology and philosophy is not itself
dependent on philosophical premises and arguments. And certainly
in the final analysis his account must be evaluated in terms of
its philosophical and theological adequacy. Neither *The Letters
to Lücke* nor this introduction to them attempts these tasks. It
will suffice here to clear the path for just such work.

Schleiermacher's Christology

The criticisms of Schleiermacher's Christology made by his
reviewers are similar in structure to those concerning his doctrine of God. Indeed, in *The Letters to Lücke*, Schleiermacher
discusses his doctrine of Christ within the context of his understanding of God-consciousness. Ferdinand Christian Baur had
charged that Schleiermacher's Christology was based upon philosophical speculation rather than historical data. Primary for
Schleiermacher, he contended, was the idea of redemption, which
is in a secondary and derivatory sense applied to the historical
Jesus.[65] In fact, Baur accused Schleiermacher of replacing the
historical Jesus with a philosophically constructed ideal Christ.
For this reason Baur called Schleiermacher a gnostic.

According to Baur, Schleiermacher's decision to place Christology within the section dealing with the Christian consciousness
of grace indicates that his view of Christ is dictated by anthro-
pological rather than historical analysis. If Schleiermacher
truly believed that Jesus Christ were central for the content and
validity of his dogmatics, he would have placed Christology at the
beginning rather than in the second part of *The Christian Faith*.

Baur finds further confirmation of his interpretation in the
fact that Schleiermacher so often discusses Jesus Christ in propositions that are descriptions of human states of mind. These
discussions ralate primarily to the experience of redemption and so

to the "ideal Christ," who is known in religious self-consciousness as the redeemer. Only in the section on ecclesiology does
Schleiermacher deal with the historical Christ in propositions
expressing the constitution of the world. And these propositions,
Baur points out, could, according to Schleiermacher's own admission, be omitted altogether from dogmatics. It would seem, then,
that Schleiermacher is willing to omit the "historical foundation"
of faith, i.e., the historical Jesus Christ.

In this reference to the Introduction of *The Christian Faith*,
Baur had in fact misread Schleiermacher. As Schleiermacher explains in *The Letters to Lücke*, he had written that "the other
forms (doctrines expressing the divine attributes and the constitution of the world) cannot be excluded from a Christian doctrinal
system without causing the loss of a historical orientation and
therefore its ecclesial character."[66] In his Latin text, Baur
had mistranslated the term "historical orientation" (*geschichtliche
Haltung*) as "historical foundation" (*fundamentum historicum*).[67]
This evidence, then, is inadmissible.

Despite this correction, however, the basic issue posed by
Baur remains. And other reviewers argued in a similar vein.[68]
There was widespread suspicion that Schleiermacher treated Jesus
Christ the redeemer as a postulate derived from the need for
redemption. Both his selection and his interpretation of the gos-
pel materials were seen to be shaped by his ideal of the redeemer.

In *The Letters to Lücke*, Schleiermacher insists that his
Christology begins not with the idea of a redeemer but with empirical data: the effect of Jesus Christ on the Christian religious
self-consciousness. That effect is one of allowing God-consciousness to predominate with ease in every moment of life, and
Christians are aware that this ability is derived not from their
own efforts but from a power transmitted by Christ. In Christianity every element of the religious self-consciousness is related
to this experience. As he puts it in *The Letters to Lücke*,
"Christians have their complete consciousness of God only as it is
produced in them through Christ."[69] Since this power entered
history with the appearance of the redeemer and with the communication of his God-consciousness to others, the essence of Christianity may be said to be based on historical fact. There is an evident
parallel, then, between criticisms of Schleiermacher's doctrine of
God and his Christology. In both cases, critics contend that
philosophical premises dictated the treatment, and, in both
cases, Schleiermacher's response in the same. The primary datum,

the character of religious self-consciousness itself, leads to intellectual reflection but is not produced by it.

Even granting this insistence upon the starting point for theology, however, the critics have detected a serious issue in the interpretation of Schleiermacher's Christology. Although Schleiermacher's account of the redeemer may not rightly be called a transcendental deduction, it does rely in large measure upon an argument from what is given to religious self-consciousness to what must be presupposed about the redeemer in history.[70] The deployment of this argument from effect to cause is in need of scrutiny. Moreover, there is reason to ask how Schleiermacher's Christology squares with historical study of the life of Jesus, as carried out not only in his own *Life of Jesus* but in life of Jesus research as a whole.[71]

Indeed, Schleiermacher's reliance upon this argument in the formation of this Christology brings once again into view the twofold problematic that pervades the debates about his conception of dogmatics, his analysis of piety, and his treatment of the relationship between philosophy and theology. Is there too little or too much "philosophy" in the philosophical theology that is presented in the Introduction to *The Christian Faith*, and does that philosophical theology rightly or wrongly determine the system as a whole?

This is not the place to provide the answer to that question. This introduction has only the more modest task of calling attention to Schleiermacher's own self-understanding, as illumined by *The Letters to Lücke*. In discussing the nature of dogmatics, piety, philosophy, and theology, Schleiermacher attempts always to keep polarities together. After full consideration, Schleiermacher interpreters may have to conclude that the attempt did not succeed. Certainly many early reviewers were led to that conclusion. In any case, before a judgment can be reached, one should listen carefully to Schleiermacher's own defense testimony.

Read as a document that makes clear Schleiermacher's intentions and concerns, *The Letters to Lücke* is a valuable aid for understanding Schleiermacher at least as well as he understood himself. And since the work may lead to a better formulation of key interpretative issues, it is our hope that this translation will help spark and facilitate further inquiry.

IV.   The Text and Translation

On the <u>*Glaubenslehre*</u>: *Two Letters to Dr. Lücke* appeared
first in the journal *Theologische Studien und Kritiken* and was
later reprinted in Schleiermacher's *Sämmtliche Werke*.[72]   The best
edition of the text, however, was prepared by Hermann Mulert, and
it is upon this that the present translation is based.[73]

In his edition, Mulert included a brief Introduction and a
set of footnotes dealing mainly with bibliographical references.
This material has been of great benefit to us, but the new annota-
tions that we have supplied go considerably beyond his work both
in explanatory and in bibliographical data, especially by including
brief biographical sketches of many of the persons mentioned by
Schleiermacher. The notes are designed to provide students with
sufficient background information with which to deal with the work
and to facilitate further research on the part of scholars. Cross
references indicate first the letter and then the note; for example,
the notation "see n. II, 13" refers the reader to the Notes to the
Second Letter, number thirteen.

Mulert also divided the text of the two letters into sections
marked by editorial subheadings. Since these subheadings were few
and in some cases so lengthy that they served almost as a commentary, we have for this edition made a fresh division of the text
with our own subheadings placed in brackets.

Although portions of *The Letters to Lücke* have been translated frequently for the purpose of quotation, this edition is to
our knowledge the first translation into English of the complete
text. We have sought to render in a clear and readable idiom the
content of the German original. As befits the genre of a public
communication in the guise of a personal letter, the prose is
sometimes elevated and sometimes colloquial. Thus, although in
many cases extremely long paragraphs and sentences have been
broken up into shorter units, it has been our hope to preserve
the movement of Schleiermacher's thought and to retain as much as
possible the tone of the piece.

In this work even more than in his scholarly writings,
Schleiermacher eschewed reliance upon a highly technical vocabulary. Nonetheless, the translation of several terms deserves
comment. *Idee* has been translated as "idea," *Begriff* as "concept,"
Vorstellung as "representation," and *Gedanke* as "notion."
Schleiermacher does not make these distinctions into a matter of
philosophical principle, but he does follow the German usage that
implies a contrast between the pictorial character of *Vorstellung*
and the refined conceptuality of *Begriff*. He also freely

interchanges *Vorstellung* and *Idee*. Yet for the sake of clarity
the use of distinct English equivalents seems advisable.

The adjective *sinnlich* is used by Schleiermacher to refer to
matters pertaining to the human senses, the world of finite objects, and in general to relations of reciprocity between the
self and other objects. Thus there is much variation in corresponding English terms. For example, *das sinnliche Gefühl* is
translated as "the sensible feeling," *das sinnliche Selbstbe-
wusstsein* as "the sensible self-consciousness," and *das
Sinnenleben* as "the sensuous life."

The term *Glaubenslehre* has been rendered "doctrine of faith,"
except where Schleiermacher is referring specifically to his own
dogmatics. In those instances, the term is a title as well as a
designation of the dogmatic task, and we have left it in German.

Schleiermacher refers to his work, *Über die Religion: Reden
an die gebildeten Verächter*, as simply his *Reden über Religion* or
Reden. Accordingly, we have translated these references as the
Speeches on Religion or the *Speeches*. He speaks of his *Kurze
Darstellung des theologischen Studiums* as the *Kurze Darstellung*
or as the *Enzyklopädie*, and we have translated these references
as *The Brief Outline* and *The Encyclopedia*.

Wherever possible, we have cited and quoted from standard
English translations of Foreign language works. Many of the
titles mentioned in *The Letters to Lücke*, however, remain un-
translated, and in those cases we have cited the source directly
and, as the occasion arises, supplied our own translations of the
relevant passages. Quotations from *The Christian Faith* required
us to combine these procedures: We rely on the available English
translation of the second edition and offer our own translation
of the first edition.[74]

We welcome this opportunity to express our appreciation to
those persons who have offered us their guidance and encouragement
in our Schleiermacher studies. Francis Schüssler Fiorenza is
especially grateful to Dr. Trutz Rendtorff of the University of
Munich, and James Duke is pleased to acknowledge his intellectual
indebtedness to Dr. Jack Forstman of Vanderbilt University.

Several colleagues deserve special recognition for their aid
in the preparation of this translation. Since each of us, working
independently and unaware of the other's efforts, submitted a manuscript to the editor's desk almost simultaneously, we are grateful
that Dr. Robert Ellwood, then editor of the Texts and Translations
series of the American Academy of Religion, supported the strategm

of a collaboration. We consider ourselves fortunate to have been
able to benefit from the suggestions of such keen readers as Dr.
Robert Scharlemann and Dr. Charles Wood. Double thanks are due
Dr. Richard Crouter, who was willing to review the manuscript
at two different stages of its drafting. Dr. James A. Massey,
the present editor of the Texts and Translations series, has given
invaluable assistance in readying the work for publication. We
are grateful also to the Nineteenth Century Theology Working
Group of the American Academy of Religion for its sponsorship of
the project. Full responsibility for any remaining defects in
the final product should be placed upon us alone.

                    James Duke and Francis Schüssler Fiorenza
                    December, 1979

THE FIRST LETTER

[The Purpose of the Letter]

At last, my dear friend, I managed to set aside for myself enough time that I can say that the quills were almost already sharpened and the paper readied for me to begin on the second edition of my *Glaubenslehre*.[1] But the closer I came to the task, the more hampered I felt by its difficulties.[2] As you know, I have often mentioned how uncertain an author feels in such a situation and how difficult it is to decide how many liberties may be taken with a book that in its present form has already found acceptance and become public property. Of course, this probably applies more to works that belong to or touch upon the area of art than to scholarly writings. If I had completely changed my view and so written a new book that refuted my first one by passing over it, or even if I had decided that essential changes were necessary in certain sections, then someone else would be free to defend the old work against me and indeed to republish it in its original form. This would not concern me at all, once I had explained that the work no longer represented my teaching and opinion. And therefore I would have even felt free to make whatever changes I saw fit.

But the shoe pinched me elsewhere, and I saw myself in a situation unlike any I had been in before. When a work which sets forth one's teaching has been reviewed so often and from such diverse viewpoints and has received such different sorts of criticism, it becomes increasingly difficult--as I very soon realized--to retain that total impartiality necessary for a successful reexamination and revision of the book. Instead of focusing on the various sections and their interrelations, in short, instead of immersing oneself totally in the work itself, one's glance is always diverted outward. This person and that person float before one's mind, first at one passage and then at another. Should this point be defended or should that one be corrected? But then the unity and simplicity of the work would necessarily suffer.

If I had imagined beforehand that this revision would be as difficult as I now find it to be, instead of promising to produce a revised edition, I would have long ago authorized the publisher to reissue unchanged as many copies as he considered useful and necessary.[3] Yes, even now I would ask him to do just that and to

release me from my promise at least for a few years until the
amazing cacophony of voices has quieted and the book has been
eclipsed by more recent publications. But I was afraid that in the
meantime I might have died and so would have done nothing for my
book.

Since I must now start to work, I know of no other way to
gain the necessary impartiality and calm than to pour out my heart
about various matters beforehand, and for that purpose I have
selected you. You see, it is a service of true friendship that
I am asking from you. And, in imposing upon you to hear me out,
I do not at all want to presume that you yourself would be in
total agreement with my *Glaubenslehre* or to demand that you should
step into the breach in its defense. I want only to give you an
account of what I am thinking of doing in this second edition,
and what not, and why, so that, once I have decided what I am not
able to do, I will be able to put the matter out of my mind as I
work.[4]

[Posture Towards Mistaken Criticisms]

First, then, I should confess to you that a friend's question
has been ringing in my ears for a long time, and it has become
increasingly disturbing: how in this second edition do I intend
to handle my opponents? I did not know how to get rid of the
question, even though it does not at all correspond to my intentions. In general I acknowledge opponents only in matters of
intentions and deeds. The thinker has only co-workers, the author
has only readers, and I know of no other relations between them.
If I had written my book with the intention of founding a sect
or school, then I could have opponents. But I know that I had
no such thing in mind. And even if now and then someone has imputed this intention to me, he still remains for me only a reader,
although one upon whom I have made an impression that I did not
intend to make, because it is not true. An author indeed owes it
to his readers to make his book as good as he possibly can, but
nothing more. When a reader writes something about my book, then
of course the relationship is reversed. He does not have a
greater right than any other author to demand that I read his
work. And, if I become his reader, I do not owe him anything but
to make the best possible use of his book. Of some sort of obligation to reply to objections and to become a writer again for the
sake of those readers who have written, I know nothing at all.

Therefore, if any of my so-called opponents had completely
convinced me, say, that my work is self-contradictory,[5] or that

faith in God is inconsistent with the position I have expounded,[6] or that I make the Christian faith dependent on fantasy,[7] or, what is perhaps in essence the same, that I want to reintroduce paganism into Christianity,[8] or even that my *Glaubenslehre* is perfectly compatible with the papal system of the Roman church[9]--if even one of these arguments had been proved true, there would have been no mention of a second edition of my *Glaubenslehre*. Instead, I would have sought a convenient opportunity to renounce it. Likewise, if on individual points my critics had taught me something, the fruits of their instruction would certainly not have been left out of my revised edition, although the more corrections there would have been, the more inappropriate I would have considered it to cite individually each of those who instructed me.

Even less can I acknowledge an obligation to refute objections which in my opinion miss the point or are based on misunderstandings. An author does not owe this to the critics, who deal with the subject matter all the time and therefore can come to their own conclusions. Equally little does the author owe it to the republic, for it has the documents before it, and each person is free to make up his own mind. For that matter I do not know why my readers as a whole should have any more rights than each individual reader. It would be a different situation of course if the two parties, my critics and I, were to appear together in a large public forum. Then indeed I can imagine that, after my critics had spoken, many voices would rise from the audience demanding that I too should speak. It would then be difficult not to obey them. But I would be greatly embarrassed because I would not know at the outset what my actual social status was with my critics. Despite their many attestations of respect, do they not in fact make charges against me, such as those mentioned above and others, which are actually incompatible with any respect? Or can I deserve even the slightest respect when I preach, as they know I do, or even hold a preaching office, at the same time as I advocate such views as those alledged to be found in my *Glaubenslehre*? Our friend in Bonn is especially severe in this respect.[10] But he is by no means the only one, for many others, equally respectable, have shown themselves to be equally severe. Even in such an assembly I would scarcely know what to say except to implore them for their own sakes to be true to themselves. And if they consider me to be so disreputable, they should not at all spare me, but greet me with whatever labels they feel I deserve. They should refrain from praising me and should apply the term *summe*

venerandus[11] just as it is and without any embellishment only to
my doctorate in theology.

The best that can be said of me is that I am not what they
take me to be. Nor would I probably say anything more, except
perhaps to say to those who have made contradictory charges
against me--for example, one calls me a gnostic;[12] another, an
Alexandrian,[13] which is the opposite of a gnostic; one traces my
thought back to Schelling;[14] another, to Jacobi;[15] one claims I
teach the principles of monastic morality,[16] whereas another considers me a Cyrenian, even though he does not explicitly say
so[17]--to these persons I could only say that they should first
come to agree among themselves, an apt piece of advice for such
situations, which a friend recently used with good success in a
similar debate with opponents. More ought not be expected of
me by all those persons whose opinion of my work actually assumes
that I am either too stupid to notice the contradictions into
which my whole life has fallen, or so frivolous as to be pleased
with being caught in them because I do not take anything seriously,
or so despicable as to be unable to make a living except in a
profession which must actually be utterly repugnant to me.

However, even if I were willing to overlook such presuppositions, there are still other reasons of a different sort why I
cannot bring myself to reply to these critics and to others.
Very many of their objections are based solely on the fact that
statements have been imputed to me which I have never expressed
and could never acknowledge as mine. Indeed, in some cases I
have actually stated the very opposite. For example, how does
our Delbrück come to assume that my teaching would allow for
regeneration outside the Christian church?[18] Is it really possible
that he could have glanced even cursorily at the sections on this
doctrine? How can Mr. Rust conclude from a passage where I state
that the God of my childhood has vanished from me that I have retained a childish form of piety?[19] And in the final analysis he
tries to explain my whole system from this perspective![20]

Another respected scholar, but from the Tübingen school,
wants to demonstrate that I place the historical Christ in the background from what I am said to have taught about Christ as the Logos
of God apart from his appearance in a particular person.[21]
But this representation occurs nowhere in my book, and our friend
Nitzsch has quite correctly noted that this representation is included among those ecclesiastical concepts that I had already excluded from my system.[22] Perhaps, however, this theologian has
walked along the same pathway with Professor Baur who, because I

speak of the archetypal and the historical in Christ, attributes
to me a double Christ, an archetypal and an historical. He then
contends that the latter, of which I always and exclusively speak,
is greatly subordinated to the former.[23] Indeed this suspicion
seems all the more plausible since Klaiber claims that I stated
it was necessary for an inner Christ to appear *also* in a historical person (contrary to my custom I must underline the word "also"
because the accent falls on it), as if there were even a trace in
my work of an inner Christ prior to the historical Christ.[24]

Indeed, whenever members of the Tübingen school comment on my
Glaubenslehre, their remarks are extraordinarily rich in such
insinuations and innuendoes. What I have expressly stated against
such idealistic nonsense (you need compare only the *Tübinger
Zeitschrift*, 1:251) has been twisted around into support of it.[25]
And when nothing else works, then the line of argument is taken
that, since my statements do not refute Baur's presupposition,
then his presupposition must also be mine. Indeed, in two different essays from this school I have had to read that, according
to my teaching, the communication of the sinlessness and perfection of Christ occurs by teaching and example, even though I have
stated the very opposite (vol. 2, p. 213).[26] Now when such
statements as the following are attributed to me, for example,
the "there could be nothing in the historical part of the
Glaubenslehre that was not already present in the ideal or philosophical parts,"[27] or "that I postulate three moments in the idea
of God,"[28] two of which are so poorly conceived that they are not
even mutually exclusive, or that I "distinguish between a God
who is above all change and a God who is subject to time,"[29]
then I do not feel obliged to embroil myself in this school's
controversy with a Schleiermacher whom I in no way recognize as
myself.

Furthermore, if everything is made dependent upon the life of
Christ in us, whoever can conclude that the death of Christ and
with it the whole historical person of Christ must appear superfluous is employing a logic that I cannot understand.[30] Despite
my great respect for Dr. Steudel, it grieves me to have to say
the same thing about his conjecture that, if I had lived in that
day, my teaching could have enticed me into Mohammedanism,[31]
since he has substituted for what I call the fusion of the sensible
and the higher self-consciousness the Islamic covenant of reconciliation between the two. Indeed, this objection completely
disappears if one takes into account what is said about Mohammedanism in my Introduction.[32]

[Relation Between Knowledge and Piety]

In other cases I do not know how to deal with the criticisms
because the basis of the disagreement, when it is not a mere ver-
bal dispute, seems to lie far too deep for me to resolve it. This
is how I feel about Dr. Bretschneider. The disagreement that he
first notes seems to me to be very easily resolved. This theologian denies that feeling and self-consciousness are identical
by reminding me that there are unconscious feelings.[33] The problem
here is simply that he uses the expression "feeling" differently
than I do, even though we agree on the meaning of the term "self-
consciousness." If I would concede that the expression "feeling"
can be used in the sense he does, and if I would then state that
his explanation of consciousness as a knowledge of every actual
mode of determination of our being coincides with what I mean by
self-consciousness, except that I would not like to use the term
"knowledge" in this case, then the disagreement between us would
not arise until later. I think that everyone knows that I place
little weight on definitive terminology so long as I am convinced
that I mean the same thing as the other person. But then the real
disagreement between us lies in Dr. Bretschneider's conviction
that, in the area to which piety belongs, this determination of
our being, and therefore our knowledge of this determination, depends primarily upon the conception of ideas, because feeling can
refer only to what has already become an object of thought.[34]
I can take him only to mean that one must first have to conceive
the idea of God before one can come to the knowledge of that
determination of one's being. Of course, I must completely reject
this opinion. But at the outset I need only to state that I do
not consider a prior conception of the idea of God to be piety because that conception is not a knowledge of the mode of determination of my being, nor does it develop first out of that knowledge.
So, once again, the dispute would seem to be over the meaning of
a word.

Upon closer inspection, however, the difference between Dr.
Bretschneider and myself lies so deeply rooted that I have little
hope for resolving it, since I have actually done all that I could
for that purpose. I would therefore be forced only to restate in
other words what I have already said. I think first of all that
well-known Egyptian monk who was brought to the brink of despair
when it was demanded that he no longer think of God as having a
bodily form.[35] This monk certainly had not independently conceived
the idea of God that Dr. Bretschneider has in mind, but, indeed,
because of his own lack of ability, he had even corrupted the

traditional representation of the supreme being. Does one want
to deny the poor man the possibility that his piety could have been
purer and better than his idea, even if what is felt can refer only
to an object of thought? And when there are so many thousands of
people whose representations of God, even though they are not as
crude, are still highly imperfect, yet whose piety is simply and
pure, may I then not believe that piety as the determination of
the self-consciousness could be present even before one has come
to a concept of the idea of God? And if I were not to appeal also
to the awareness of freedom as a self-consciousness, will one say
that there can be no such consciousness until the idea of freedom
has first been conceived and that whoever has not conceived this
idea of freedom could not act as one self-consciously free?

And, if in contrast to this picture of my monk, I put forward
the example of a group of intellectuals who have conceived the
idea of God and who, as they do with every other important idea,
have worked it out intellectually and drawn the consequences from
it, but whose feeling for the idea never emerges and never makes
any impact on their lives, should I nevertheless not be allowed
to say that the conception of the idea of God, considered in and
by itself, is not part of piety and is not necessarily the first
element in piety?[36] But is it not true, dear friend, that I have
said all this many times before? Why then the repetition? In my
opinion the arguments in the case between my critic and myself
are closed. Each person must examine and decide the issue for
himself. Further reiteration would be only a repetition.

I do not know whether you have come across similar remarks in
the late Tzschirner's *Briefe eines Deutschen*. The case is much
the same as that above. When he claims that the most basal element
in piety is not feeling any more than knowing or doing, but disposition, it would seem that he coordinates the first three with
one another, but wants to characterize the last as more inward and
as higher.[37] But I do not locate what I call feeling where he
does, but where he places disposition, and I do not use this term
only because in current parlance it has a predominantly practical
connotation. Yet, when I reflect on how pious persons are inclined to connect all their affections with their consciousness of
God and as it were to dissolve them in it, then this distinctive
mode of feeling, from which corresponding ways of thinking and
acting develop, obviously constitutes one's disposition. It
would then appear that the dispute between us could be very easily
resolved.

However, when I again observe how even this admirable gentleman seems to believe that feeling always follows from a representation and, as he clearly states, that the ultimate foundation of
faith always rests on the insight into the necessary interrelation
among comprehended ideas, then I must repeat that what I understand as pious feeling is not derived from a representation, but
is the original expression of an immediate existential relationship.[38] Thus I find myself again opposing the same position here
as in the case of Dr. Bretschneider.

I am sure, dear friend, that you regret as deeply as I do the
untimely death of the liberal and vigorous Tzschirner.[39] And so
you will also give me credit for acknowledging Dr. Bretschneider's
manifold merits. Consequently, when I try to communicate to you
what I believe to be the basis of the differences between these
men and myself, you will not take this to mean that I intended
to say anything disparaging about them.

In our great church fellowship there are certainly many
theologians who have dedicated themselves to their profession before they themselves had experienced much Christian piety in
their own lives. That I consider this to be a shortcoming can be
learned by anyone who has glanced at my *Encyclopedia* even once.[40]
Nevertheless, I recognize that this is unavoidable in the present
state of affairs. Therefore, it is truly gratifying when many
of these persons are gradually led to a lively Christian piety as
a consequence of their intellectual work with theological subjects. But, as the late Semler remarked,[41] they should not regard
their particular experience as the general norm, as another
famous theologian has done by asserting that "religion is the
daughter of theology."[42] This assertion must be rejected by
those who have experienced piety in their youth before they even
had any thought of their future vocation and who, therefore, know
from their own particular history that piety is independent of
every insight into any system of comprehended ideas.

I too object to that assertion, and in doing so, even though
I do not use the same language as they do, I am doing nothing
other than what a large school has done for more than a century.
But should not every one of us reject that assertion? Even if it
can now no longer be stated as a rule that piety remains hidden
to the wise, do we not have every reason to thank God that he has
revealed piety to the immature especially, that is, to those
whose piety would not amount to much at all if it were to be based
upon a *complexus* of ideas? Was not even our Luther such a person,
and did he not begin to reflect about his piety only when he was

hard pressed to strengthen his possession of it, so that his
theology is plainly a daughter of his religion? And how would
our evangelical church fare if living evangelical Christianity
had not struck such deep roots in unspeculative and unphilosophi-
cal persons whose piety is so far from being based on thought and
grounded in an insight into a system of ideas that by and large
they came only gradually to think about their piety? Thanks be to
God, many others now share my conviction that our piety is not
really that different from that of such persons after all.

The previously mentioned position, however, presupposes that
those who are unable to be affected inwardly first by an object
of thought and, as would have to be the case here, to grasp a set
of ideas other than those related to their own concerns either
have no piety at all or have only a piety derived from that of
the theologians rather than from their own personal lives. If so,
there would then emerge a hierarchy of intellectual cultured, a
priesthood of speculation, which I for my part cannot find to be
very Protestant and which, whenever I had the fate to encounter
it, has never appeared without a certain popish tinge. Moreover,
this position naturally entails a different view of the ministry
of the Word. It makes every Christian sermon into an instruction,
and, indeed, not only insofar as Scripture must be explained to
the people because it comes to us in a foreign language and from
a foreign age, but also because it tries to lead persons into this
complex of ideas by gradual steps.

Others of us, however, see the task of ministry as that of
giving a clear and enlivening description of a common inner experience, and what emerges as doctrinal teaching is really only a
preparation and a means to this end. We do not fancy that we are
introducing into our church communities something completely new,
as though in the first course of study we communicate the ideas
to them and then in a second course we base piety on the ideas.
Rather, what is possessed is shared in common, and we serve our
brothers only by explaining more clearly to them what it is and so
awaken in them the joy in it as well as concern for it.

Likewise, the two positions very naturally come to differ
with regard to the conception of dogmatics. The first position
understands dogmatics to be a conjoining of the ideas from which
piety should then emerge. Or perhaps dogmatics is expected to
prove these ideas, for the late Tzschirner expressly complains
that the method I chose scarcely allows a proof.[43] But I know
nothing about such ideas and even less about proofs for them,

and I do not know where a dogmatics would come from unless piety
were already present.

At this point, dear friend, I am reminded of an essay published in a newly-founded journal which preludes about this theme.
It accuses me of confusing the practical application of dogmatics
for theological skill [*Kunst*] with dogmatics proper.[44] Now surely
this is only another quarrel over a word, for I have said clearly
enough that my dogmatics does not claim to be anything more than
dogmatics. Therefore, anyone who demands that dogmatics should
eliminate every positive element as mere historical trapping and
should seek only the pure truth of a universal rational faith is
using the word "dogmatics" differently than I am. Indeed, I have
long since made it known that I doubt if such a thing can even be
produced.

What now calls to mind this essay, which even you yourself,
if you recall, found less than clear and solid, is this. The
author seeks to write a piece that will serve so-called natural
religion--I am sorry but I cannot express myself otherwise--in the
same way that dogmatics serves the Christian religion, in that
he tries to derive the pure truth of an independent rational faith
from the original, pure feeling of humanity.[45] Now I like to
console myself that this (only incidentally hinted at) sublimation
of my method into this airy region will not produce any dangerous
or destructive sublimate, but rather nothing at all.

But the notion of basing piety upon an insight into a complex
of ideas which have been learned is another issue entirely. For
if, as this author puts it, the positive is constructed by philosophy, and if those doing the construction can condescend to look
long enough at those poor folk who cannot at all comprehend the
relation between speculation and their piety, they must finally
admit to each other that their speculation could not have constructed the positive unless it had already found the positive
present.[46] Piety, then, as it is actually found, is ungrounded,
arbitrary, accidental, and so nothing, and therefore philosophy
can for the sake of its own honor have nothing to do with it.
If the unfortunate result is that philosophy reigns alone in those
frigid polar regions to which only a few can penetrate and that
piety does not develop from ideas at all, then there is reason to
fear than many noble persons, especially the young, will abandon
piety out of respect for philosophy and leave piety to the ignorant.
For the sake of these persons, however, others of us will persist
and seek to clarify and strengthen their piety, not by means of
proofs and ideas, but by means of the ancient indemonstrable

logos.[47] But I feel sorry for those who, if they had not been led
astray, could have given us excellent help. But I will return to
my original subject from which I digressed and ask whether you are
more confident than I am that by debating over a single point we
can resolve such a deep-rooted and far-ranging dispute, which in
reality can be resolved only by activity, by exhausting the
energies of the contending parties, or by calm and prolonged deli-
berations. I am sure you will answer in the negative and therefore will approve of my silence.

[Misunderstandings about the Feeling of Dependency]

Surely you will also find it natural that I do not feel
obliged to deal with the strangest misunderstandings for which with
the best conscience I can assert that I am not at fault. Or do
you think that it might still be worthwhile to add a special section to my original explanations so that no one could still believe that absolute dependence upon God destroys human freedom?[48]
Were you to request it, I could only despair, for I do not know
how I could express myself any more clearly than I already have.
But I also believe that further explanation is now even less necessary, since anyone who still thinks that human freedom has to be
conceived in such a way as to be irreconcilable with absolute dependence will find that position reflected in the theologian from
Württemberg whose position I was thinking of previously.[49] In
this controversy he has taken the position that the will of the
Almighty that free beings should also exist outside of God constitutes in itself an inexplicable act of divine self-limitation.[50]
If I had claimed that this conclusion results from rejecting my
position, then that familiar outcry against sophistic dialectics
or fabricated consequences would have been raised. But since this
unpretentious man has been troubled by his logical conscience and
has taken the courage to say it quite explicitly, surely I should
be allowed to accept it as useful. And so I think that the die
has been cast on this issue and each person can choose for himself.
Those who can imagine a God who performs acts of self-limitation
can also flatter themselves into believing in a freedom that
raises itself above absolute dependence. Those, however, who cannot reconcile themselves to such acts of God, and I freely confess
my inability to do so, should sacrifice the representation of an
"absolute freedom over against absolute dependence"--a representation that I can in no way admit.

But there are still other misunderstandings about the feeling
of absolute dependence that place me in the same situation.

I wholeheartedly concede to Dr. Steudel that in acknowledging our
dependence we also specify our view of the world.[51] And I hope
that a large part of my *Glaubenslehre* is nothing other than a
description of this world view. Indeed, if I were to complete my
christliche Sittenlehre, it would be from beginning to end nothing
other than the description of how the acknowledgment of our absolute dependence shapes the determination of our will.[52] But I
simply cannot see how it can thereby be concluded that piety does
not have its place more immediately in feeling than in volition
or knowledge,[53] because piety is that acknowledgment itself,
and from this issue the pious view of the world and pious determinations of the will (to use Steudel's very own terms). In thinking of this passage, it dawns on me that I could be misunderstood
to be saying that piety is not the acknowledgment itself, but the
"accepting of pleasure and pain and the submitting to fate en-
gendered in this acknowledgment."[54] But in my opinion this is
already a pious determination of the will and way of acting.
Consequently, I am not at all aware of having in any way occasioned such a misunderstanding.

But how should I respond when an absolutely dependent being
is judged to be questionable because it could not coexist with the
view that as free beings we have to actualize the divine order of
the world and that this actualization is to be a relationship of
mutual interaction with God?[55] Furthermore, "whoever is conscious
of being 'merely' absolutely dependent"--though the word 'merely'
was not manufactured by me--"would no longer be a self."[56] And
when Dr. Bretschneider tells me that, without an idea of the good,
the feeling of absolute dependence would be nothing but fear and
horror and that Christianity could not be founded on such a
basis--"founded" should in any case be changed to read "explained,"
since I do not speak of a "founding" at all--he must have forgotten
that at this point my explanation dealt with every kind of piety,
even the lowest type, which can express itself only as fear and
horror.[57]

Of course, I do not like to use the term "obscure" with reference to feeling because it is usually applied to representations.[58]
But even if at this level the feeling of absolute dependence (so
long as the referent is still undetermined) is said to be "obscure," not every "obscure" feeling can be called piety because
not every feeling expresses an absolute dependence.[59] But, of
course, Bretschneider means that absolute dependence would have to
be referred to the world as well as to God because much in nature

does not allow any counter-effect.[60] Consequently, many "obscure"
feelings could be identified with piety--but not in my sense of
the word!

How could anyone possibly deduce from my statements that
freezing or sweating prove an absolute dependence? Yet it is obvious from this that, in Bretschneider's opinion, since feeling is
always only an expression of a present restraint, it can only
express a relative dependence.[61] This is indeed true of the sensible feeling on which the spiritual feeling develops, but it is
not true for the spiritual feeling itself. Even stranger is the
misunderstanding that what I describe as the restraint of the
higher life is to be explained as the "desire to form one's own
personal or individual sensuous life," almost as though I had declared temporal existence per se to be apostasy, since I always
find apostasy to be present only when God-consciousness is excluded.[62]

What more should I add, when I encounter such a general misunderstanding that the analysis of self-consciousness set forth
in my *Glaubenslehre* is interpreted as if it were intended to be
something other than simply and straight forwardly empirical![63]
It was this misunderstanding that led Bretschneider to object that
my theory of original sin is inconsistent because it is really
empirical. Tell me, is it really not sufficiently clear that,
when I speak of the consciousness of sin, the need for redemption,
and the contentment that we find in Christ, I am referring to actually experienced facts and not to facts of consciousness prior to
experience? Is it not already indicated by the motto that preceeds
the text?[64] Is it not already stated in my *Encyclopedia*, which
was written before my dogmatics?[65] Honestly, it would not have
once occurred to me during a walk of a thousand miles that anyone
could understand me differently. Rather this was the one point about
which I felt perfectly carefree.

[God-Consciousness]

The last thing I ever expected was that I would be associated
at so many points with the speculative dogmaticians, among whom
I would not be able to appear even as a dilettante, for I am not
at all inclined to philosophize in dogmatics. But I am expected
to, no matter how little I want to. And how strangely it is urged
upon me! It is said that my "God-consciousness" should not be
confused with "consciousness of God," and immediately afterward
it is also said that the God-consciousness in humans is supposed
to be God itself![66] Poor me! Even when I believe I have made

every effort to be most grammatically precise, the result turns
out to be the exact opposite.

But when the terms self-consciousness, world-consciousness,
and God-consciousness are phrased in parallel form, how could it
be correct for any one to be understood differently than the
others? Is the world-consciousness in humans also the world
itself? And when I also state that God-consciousness is the being
of God in humans, must not anyone seeking to form a concept of
omnipresence acknowledge the being of God in others?[67] But is this
therefore God itself? Not any more than when I allow myself to say
that the being of Christ in us, which Christ himself mentions, is
Christ himself. You smile? As though I am supposed to have said
that, too? Indeed, it is claimed that I have. Of course, this
Christ is the ideal Christ--allegedly my sole concern--who is
both God-consciousness itself and the model of what humanity
should be.[68]

[Digression on Christ as Redeemer]

On the other hand, another view of my work--based on strange
misunderstandings and omissions that a young friend has almost
satisfactory refuted[69]--maintains that, when I smuggle in the
historical Christ, I cannot make any more of him than what
Aristotle, for example, also was.[70] Yet I am far from believing
that Professor Braniss has especially singled out this point because he knows that when it comes to speculation I do not think
primarily of him. But allow me to say a few words about this man.
Not only do I owe him thanks because he was one of the first to
deal in detail with my *Glaubenslehre*, but I also truly have a high
respect for him. I would grant him full right to oppose me, if I
had maintained what he claims I have. He has the right to demand
that I acknowledge that the historical form of redemption began
with Christ himself and also that it should be first posited in
him as a minimum. But he can demand this of me only if he agrees
with the presupposition that I have taken to be the basic presupposition of Christianity, namely, that this power is to be attributed completely and exclusively to Christ and that no trace of a
need for redemption exists in his person.[71] I hold to this presupposition so firmly that I would not allow any biblical passage
that appears to say the opposite to lead me to change my mind.[72]
The distinction between development and conflict can certainly
be maintained. But to consider as sin the self's struggle with
itself to submit to God's will is a stricture from which I cannot

dispense myself. And for that reason I cannot attribute such a
struggle to Christ without annihilating the basic presupposition.

Nevertheless, even after Christ appeared, redemption as a
fact was in actuality without effect until he acted to effect it.
Even as a historical phenomenon, therefore, redemption remained
an insignficant force as long as Christ was on earth. I would
never refuse to concede this point. But nothing can be concluded
from this admission that could serve as a ground of complaint
against me. My discussion does not also mean that the power of
redemption in Christ must have been minimal,[73] because it is only
through the divine power dwelling within him that Christ becomes
this particular historical person. Those who cannot accept this
premise will not only be unable to accomodate their way of thinking to the system of my *Glaubenslehre*, which on this point states
nothing unusual, neither will they be able to accomodate themselves to the system of the church, which so far as I know even
Braniss with full freedom adheres to. Instead, they must resort
to that view which leads to a common redemption of all through
all, in which the Christ is only one outstanding point. But how
anyone could attempt to pass off some such view as my teaching,
I can even less understand.[74]

But I return now to where I left off. With regard to my
Christology as a whole, I am content to refer anyone to what my
friend Nitzsch has testified on my behalf.[75] But this God-consciousness which is supposedly God himself, of which I have said
nothing, and this double God, one unchangeable and one subject
to time, of which I have said nothing, and these three moments
which I allegedly distinguish in the idea of God, of which I have
said nothing, all of these misunderstandings and many others of
this sort are related to my supposed pantheism, even though they
are not consistent with one another.[76]

[The Accusation Of Pantheism]

I have been challenged so often to explain my position on
pantheism that I cannot ignore the voices. Nor do I want merely
to hide behind that statement of our friend Nitzsch, who noted
that in former times Christianity was inclined towards a view
that was in a certain sense pantheistic.[77] For there may be some
truth to the warning of another theologian that we should be careful with this term because in these days ignorance plays with
nothing as much. I do not want to say it is ignorance which is at
play, since I know how unpleasant it is to be scolded. But game
enough is being played with this term.[78] Yet what am I to do when

I cannot discover where this assumption that I am a pantheist
comes from? The late Tzschirner assumes it as a well-known fact,
since when he refers to the "aesthetic principle"--a combination
of words with which I can hardly associate myself--he has me
especially in mind.[79] Moreover, he claims that this aesthetic
principle is to be explained mainly on the basis of Schelling's
philosophy, which has revived Spinoza's pantheism.

Likewise, it has been said elsewhere that my true intention
was to reinterpret and to model Christianity on pantheism, a
philosophy altogether irreconcilable to Christianity.[80] Since
this criticism is made against a person who has so loudly and so
often repeated that Christian doctrine must be presented in total
independence from any philosophical system, the allegation ought
to be substantiated with the most stringent evidence.[81] Indeed
no one should even repeat the accusation without citing such evidence. But if what I have never taught is treated as a well-known
fact, without anyone at all having proved it, what should I do?

Likewise, Dr. Bretschneider claims that I, along with Dr.
Marheinecke and Dr. Hase, am dependent upon Schelling's philosophy.
And he is of the opinion that we give evidence of this dependence
in that we consider the development of the world as an evolving
personality of God and the opposition between the individual and
the absolute as sin.[82] For my own part, I can do no more than to
protest until I am shown where one or the other opinion can be
found in my writings. The terms are certainly not mine. Dr.
Bretschneider must have had in mind quite different terms, which
he then translated into this terminology that is completely
foreign to me. But the issue would then be a question of the cor-
rectness of such a translation. I know nothing in my statements
about sin or in those about the world that could have even occasioned such a translation.

A theologian from Württemberg attributed to me the propositions
that the infinite, the divine itself, is the true essence of all
things and constitutes the immanent ground of their being and life
and that the divine infinite life consists of the mutual interaction of various attractive and expansive powers.[83] These two
propositions seem to me to be incompatible, unless the infinite
divinity itself and the divine infinite life are two completely
different things. But I am not at all in the position where I must
choose between these two propositions because neither belongs to
me. When I looked for passages in my *Speeches on Religion* that
perhaps could have occasioned even one of the two views, I found
immediately instead of the first proposition a passage that quite

clearly affirms that in God nothing can be opposed, divided, or
separated, and another passage that asserts, against the second
proposition, that the divinity divides its work into infinity.[84]
When certain statements, which come from I know not where, are
added to what I have clearly and plainly stated, and my own statements are not even asked about, what can I do but allow each person to judge how much trust can be placed in such a reporter?

Another critic reads the incidental remark in the Introduction
to my *Glaubenslehre* that there could even be a pantheistic piety--
a remark that I was obliged to make because of what I had said
about Spinoza in my *Speeches*,[85] although I myself had noted that
it is irrelevant since no form of religion is pantheistic--and he
exclaims, "Eureka! What further proof is necessary?"[86] What can
I do but to abandon to his rather strange fate this man who on
this same condition would have to be everything else--I do not
know what--in addition to what he already is? In demanding that
evidence be produced, it suffices to have done it once, for I do
not want to be guilty of having led to the production of even more
books, which will do no more to resolve the issue and will certainly not even be written as beautifully and artistically as
Delbrück's book. Would you have thought that, after the way I had
challenged him to prove that charge of Spinozism, which he had in
general so well described, he would not honestly admit that my
Speeches do not at all teach such pantheism, but would instead
repeat the same unspecified insinuations of pantheism and monism
about which I had already expressed myself, as one can read in the
Appendix that I wrote?[87]

And how astonished I had to be to see my account of God so
described. Here I had looked neither to the right nor to the left
for the help of any philosopher, but had quite simply inquired
about the feeling common to all pious Christians and had attempted
to describe this feeling in such a way so as not to distort the
one aspect whenever I sought to do justice to the other aspect.
Yet Delbrück reproduces my doctrine by a completely different
chemical process, as a strange distillation of Spinoza and Fichte,
in which one ingredient disappears from each and the residue of the
one is bonded with that of the other by an inexplicable elective
affinity![88]

My sole consolation is that I have at least as much claim to
be called an idealist [*Ichheitler*] as a pantheist [*All-Einheitler*].
But is Delbrück's explanation really the same as what I say?
Do wisdom and love also emerge in this way? Or has our Delbrück
not gotten that far into my *Glaubenslehre*?[89] Or perhaps he thinks

that the conclusion of my book is not as typical of me as the Introduction and that I therefore do not take it as seriously, despite what I said about how the two parts are related to one
another?

The verse he penned in my name is a special service of love.[90]
Does my *Glaubenslehre* in any way fail to give due honor to divine
grace? Did I not declare my opposition to the notion of necessity
in God as well as to any similarity with a freedom based on
choice, that is, a freedom grounded in vacillation and uncertain-
ty?[91] But it is impossible to answer this here, for I am not a
poet who could also compose a verse in his name. But in a well-
intended and cordial letter, which was to the best of my knowledge
free of any wisecracks, I discussed with him what I considered to
be inadequate and inconsistent in his representation of God.[92]
He responded in print, however, and again called me a Spinozistic
wit.[93] I cannot regard such a response to be in keeping with the
nature of a true gentleman. And, when Delbrück equates "created
from eternity" with "not at all created," he betrays such scant
acquaintance with the issue that it is futile to continue the
discussion.[94] But what have I gotten into here? I really did
not intend to discuss your former colleague at all. Every one
of his seven sections contains such attacks as those mentioned
here, and it is neither rewarding nor pleasurable to have to repeat the same operation so often.

I would like, however, to post a danger sign here. If
Delbrück demands that for Christianity, or really for monotheism,
the world is not only a work of God, but also an accidental work
of God--his beloved rule of faith apparently allows this--then all
those who cannot conceive of anything accidental in God should
consequently be called pantheists.[95] In this sense the majority
of thinking Christians will then be considered pantheists along
with me. And what if these persons in turn say to Delbrück:
"we can do nothing else but to regard someone who postulates something accidental in God as an atheist"? They will reach this conclusion, not because his explanation extends the name of "God"
even to fetishes, but because his explanation is to characterize
only the most perfect being. In the end it would be best for
Delbrück, too, if we did not use such words that I at least use so
reluctantly, for they always leave behind a stain, not only on
those at whom they are flung, but also on those who throw them.

I have been condemned as a pantheist on the basis of my
Speeches, solely because I wanted to show the despisers of piety
that piety was everywhere, even where they sought it least.

Therefore, I indicated its presence especially in a person whose
speculation began at that time to be idolized by some in the most
perverse manner and to be condemned by others as severely as possible. Yet almost no one had noticed his genuinely human, inwardly gentle, and most attractive personality and his deep devo-
tion to the supreme being. If I had been a more cautious person,
who always anticipated the worst from his readers, then I would
have left a little space to mention that my words provide very
little occasion for considering me a Spinozist. But given what I
am, that thought did not even occur to me.

Since that time it is not so much I as the public that has
been punished, for they are always the ones to suffer in such useless hullabaloo. It would indeed be a harsh punishment if my
book had really "contributed by its enduring momentum not insigni-
ficantly to the irritating tendency towards the doctrine of pantheism," because that would have happened completely against my
will.[96] But I do not believe that it has. This much, however,
I do know. It has at least helped to dam the current of ridicule,
to snatch at least a few souls from deadening indifference, and,
by God's will, to open their eyes to true and pure piety. With
this result I am satisfied, and I consider a divine blessing, so
that I have never for a moment regretted having written the book.
Indeed, it is clear to me that to achieve these goals the book
had to be written much as it is. Even the sophisticated tone that
prodominated in it should not be eliminated because it has success-
fully countered the false sophistication of frivolous negativism.

My *Glaubenslehre* has occasioned the suspicion of pantheism
only because of the principle that I mentioned above.[97] Allow me,
therefore, to say a few words about it. You know, dear friend,
that from the very beginning I had set for myself the task of
presenting the God-consciousness developed in the Christian Church,
as we all have it within us, in all its expressions, so that it
always appears as pure as possible in each of its individual elements and so that the individual determinations that arise in this
way and strive toward unity can be viewed together, just as feeling
itself is always the same, whether it be tied to the consciousness
of our freedom of the will, the consciousness of the natural order,
or our consciousness of the course of historical development. The
doctrine of God expounded in my dogmatics is to be explained solely
from this conception of the task. Whoever thereby thinks of some
philosophy must inevitably become confused, and I have detected
such confusion in nearly all of the more extensive reviews of my
work.

[Relation Between Theology and Philosophy]

Indeed, I must now protest against the view expressed by our
friend Nitzsch. Of all those who dealt with my *Glaubenslehre*,
he has given it the best praise as well as criticism. He criticizes me for seeking to incorporate what is distinctively
Christian into a universal religious knowledge.[98] In my opinion,
however, such a knowledge would be nothing other than an abstrac-
tion from what is Christian. And even if that term is used to
refer to a speculative knowledge of God, in my work speculative
knowledge and Christianity always remain separate from each other
because I am convinced that, although Christianity and speculation
must be in harmony, they do not belong together and are not determined by each other. I have been most careful not to deviate
even a hair's breadth from this rule. Instead, on this basis
alone I have set forth not only my own propositions, but even
all my criticisms of previous formulations.

Indeed, I have never been satisfied with these formulations.
Even if one wants to call the customary treatment of the doctrine
of the divine attributes over the last century church doctrine--
and I cannot object to that term in view of my own linguistic
usage--I know that in the course of my own development I have not
come closer to this doctrine, but have moved ever more definitely
away from it. Its propositions are a mishmash of Leibnitzian-
Wolffian rational theology and quotations distilled from the Old
Testament, so that what is truly Christian is almost totally lost,
buried beneath both of them.[99] Its untenable combination of the
moral and metaphysical attributes is mainly at fault for the entry
that French atheism has made among us. For, whenever people among
us have lost interest in knowing of God, it has always been due
to the prevailing exposition rather than to the idea itself. This
is the experience that has ever more impressed itself upon me
since my youth. I have never needed a rational theology for my
piety, either to nourish it or to understand it. And I have had
just as little need of the sensuous theocracy of the Old Testament.
Consequently, I have always formed my own understanding in polemic
against that method, if it even deserves to be called a method.

Even if I had not entered the academic teaching profession--
and I could not have expected to do so because I had never previously wanted to--I would have retained this section of my dogmatics for myself and would have used it as a guide for my teaching from the pulpit. Indeed, traces of it can be found even in
my earliest sermons. Now, however, it must finally come out all

at once. If you were to ask me whether I would admit that according to my own testimony the first section of my doctrine of God belongs to the area of individual personal belief, which might have a place in the church, but according to my own theory is not due a place in dogmatics, I would answer "no." If the prevailing treatment is really church doctrine, then it must be obviously mine that is heterodox. I am firmly convinced, however, that my position is an inspired heterodoxy that in due time will eventually become orthodox, although certainly not just because of my book and perhaps not until long after my death.

As much as it may now appear as though philosophy wants to overpower Christianity and take it over by force, the healthy life of our church will nevertheless increasingly push all human speculation back into its proper sphere. No matter how many of our most well-meaning clergy return to the language of the Old Testament and preach out of the Old Testament, it will become increasingly demonstrated in this area, too, that in Christ the old has passed away and everything has become new. No matter how many theologians--and I greet them as brothers and with the greatest respect--may still attempt to clean and to polish the old method, it will become increasingly evident that formulations which supposedly belong together but simply do not can only be dead formulations. Likewise, a doctrine of God that takes its colors primarily from the pre-Christian era and derives its layout from some philosophical school cannot be accepted as a valid and correct exposition of Christian consciousness.

Therefore, I stand by my method. I confidently present my dogmatics, even this first part, as a Christian doctrine of faith. I do not believe that the protest against it will be very successful. Of course, the misunderstandings that have arisen have led me to have certain wishes for the second edition of my *Glaubenslehre*. Yet, after deliberating long and hard, I have decided that, considering everything, I cannot allow myself to make them. For today, however, you have had enough to hear. We will save that for the next time.

THE SECOND LETTER

[The Purpose of the Letter]

I wanted to tell you about my wishes for the second edition
of my *Glaubenslehre*. I do hope you have correctly understood my
somewhat casual remark, and so do not expect anything more than
an informal account of what I had previously intended to do, but
later rejected for fear that it would prove detrimental to the
book. I spoke of "wishes" because I have placed myself in the
shoes of my readers. This is especially an obligation for one
who wants to have a right to allow them so few rights as I have
recently noted.

[The Question about Reorganizing the *Glaubenslehre*]

The first desideratum is a very old one. Ever since I first
conceived the work, I have debated whether I should arrange the
parts as I did or should reverse them, beginning with what is now
the second part and concluding with the present first one.[1]
As I hope you will soon see, I have left them as they were. Surely, it would have been natural and proper for a theologian who
comes from the reformed tradition and who does not believe that
this tradition should be put aside even in the present state of
church union to have followed much more closely the outline of
the Heidelberg Catechism.[2]

Of course, a catechism is not the same as a dogmatic theology.
Therefore, I saw no harm in following a procedure in my dogmatics
that I would fault in a catechism.[3] Catechisms are designed primarily for young people, who have neither the personal experience
nor the personal knowledge of human nature that would make them
very sensitive to the need for salvation. But the basic feeling
of each and every mature and enlightened Christian must be the
ancient one that is given to humans by no other salvation [*Heil*]
and in no other name, although there can always be a great variety
of ways of representing it. Would it not, therefore, have been
most natural and orderly for me to begin from this point and to
view everything from this perspective, especially since I have so
definitely asserted that Christians have their complete consciousness of God only as it is produced in them through Christ?[4]
The doctrine of God itself would in no way be shortchanged. But
the Father would have been perceived first in Christ. The first
definite statements about God would have been that, in sending

55

Christ, God renews the human race and establishes the spiritual
Kingdom in us. The first divine attributes would have been wisdom
and love. In short, the entire doctrine would have been treated
as it is now, but in reverse order. Since the consciousness of
sin is still an element of the Christian's pious self-consciousness, the representations of divine holiness and justice would
likewise have been developed as elements of that consciousness of
God. What is now the first section, dealing mainly with the so-
called metaphysical and natural attributes of God, would have
come last.

[Misunderstandings Caused by the Present Organization]

I have been for a long time undecided whether to follow that
outline or the book's present outline, and there is good enough
reason for me to return to the question. I see quite clearly how
the present outline has been misunderstood. Most of my critics
began with the presupposition that a work organized as mine
necessarily has an anticlimatic ending. Or is it not true that the
Introduction has been regarded as the main subject and core of the
book, although it was intended only as a preliminary orientation
which, strictly speaking, lies outside of the discipline of dogmatics itself? And then what follows is obviously the first part!

Some have concluded from the nature of the propositions in
the Introduction that my dogmatics is actually a philosophy and
that it intends to demonstrate or deduce Christianity, insofar as
my position can be considered Christian at all.[5] Moreover, especially from their reading of this first part, some critics have
constructed what they regard as my pantheism.[6] In the Introduction
there is found what even Nitzsch characterizes as a certain inclination of Christianity towards this mode of representation.[7]

My critics also contend that, except for the Introduction,
only the section on sin represents my own thought. The rest of
the work is only external, an appendix, which attempts to assimi-
late as much as possible into pantheistic philosophy those church
doctrines that cannot be bypassed altogether. This interpretation
of my book has been almost universal, and, since no one enjoys
being so completely misunderstood, you will not blame me for saying
that I am almost sorry that I organized the book as I did.

Of course, I cannot really blame myself. How could I ever
have dreamed that anyone would approach my book with such a
presupposition? After all, a scientific work is not a dinner
party where the host first passes around the best wine in the hope

that the intoxication it produces will make more palatable the
inferior vintages that are brought in later. In fact, I had
consciously done my best to ensure that such an interpretation
would not arise. I had stated clearly enough that the first part,
though truly a part of the structure itself, was only a portal
and entrance hall and the propositions there, insofar as they
could be set forth in an Introduction, could be no more than out-
lines that would be filled in with their true content from the
ensuing discussion.[8]

Would I not be justified, then, in postponing this complex
of propositions until later, when their full meaning could be set
forth all at once? Indeed, an omnipotence, the aim and motive
force of which I do not know, an omniscience, the structure and
value of its contents I do not know, and an omnipresence, of which
I do not know what it emits from itself and attracts to itself,
are merely vague and barely living ideas. It is quite different
when omnipotence makes itself manifest in the consciousness of
the new spiritual creation, omnipresence in the activity of the
divine spirit, and omniscience in the consciousness of divine
grace and favor.

I had hoped, of course, that even in its present form the
book would not for a moment put off the readers with such empty
representations. I presumed--and I did not fail to say so--that
all would somehow bring along with them in their immediate self-
consciousness what was missing, so that no one would feel shortchanged, even though the content was not presented in dogmatic
form until later.[9] But all these hints were overlooked because,
as I said, many who took an interest in the book (and they should
have taken an interest in it) did not bring with them anything
that they would not receive first from dogmatics. Should I not
have rather begun my work with a description of Christian consciousness in its entirety?

When so many eminent and respected voices warn that my God
ought not to be regarded as the God of the Christian faith, I
must surmise that the Introduction and the first part must have
served as such a strange and unusual brew to intoxicate them that
the readers could no longer taste in the second part what is well
known and familiar to them.[10] To others the second part seemed
too orthodox for them to decide to take it seriously, especially
since they were vexed that someone who in their opinion appeared
perhaps even further removed from church doctrine than themselves
could still wear its mantle with a certain natural grace. They
were just as quick to take the prophetic doctrines literally as

they were to pass over the earlier materials, and I attribute
their haste to the natural curiosity of the child in us who
fears death.

[Advantages of Reorganization]

My book would not have received this kind of treatment if I
had followed the other organizational plan. No one could have
failed to recognize that the description of the consciousness
distinctive to Christianity is in truth and in actuality the real
aim of the book. Indeed, even if the Introduction were to remain
just as it is and so were to lead many to suspect that the book
was intended to be a philosophical construction, I believe that
their suspicion would vanish as soon as they were to read the
actual beginning of the work, because it would be evident that the
Introduction is not the beginning, but something altogether different. Furthermore, if the propositions now in the first part,
which in their present form serve only as an external work, were
to follow the Christology, the doctrine of the church, and the
exposition of the divine love and wisdom, they would certainly
take on a warmer tone and likewise appear in their specifically
Christian perspective. That would have been an obvious and decided improvement. If I had separated the dangerous Introduction
more clearly and sharply from the body of the work, I surely
would have prevented that most serious and glaring misunderstanding that detects in my *Glaubenslehre* a speculative tendency and
a speculative foundation.

I confess to you not only that I have been fondly attached
to this alternative arrangement for a long time but that I still
am. My decision to organize the book as I did meant that I had
to sacrifice greatly my inclination. The arrangement would have
made it more necessary to trace each doctrine back to the Chris-
tain center of self-consciousness, and as a result the distinctive
character of my book would have been highlighted at every point.
My listeners, moreover, would have received something that not
merely repeated but supplemented my lectures to them.

Just think, my dear friend, how few of those who sit before
us in the lecture halls will afterwards remain oriented towards
academics. And when we think how coldly and drily they will apply
what they have learned as dogma when they preach, we cannot fail
to note that our educational program and the future course of our
students' lives are not very well adapted to each other. Therefore, as you know, I disagree with those who think we spend too
much time on dogmatics, and I do not have a very high regard for

a so-called practical dogmatics, no matter what system it follows.
Nor would I advise that we take a different approach in our lectures on dogmatics and combine our discussions of the doctrines
of faith with some ascetic use of them or indeed turn them into
a *collegium pietatis*.[11]

During the time our students pursue their theological education, the pure scientific content of theology should not be
slighted. We, especially, are called upon to plant and nurture
this seed whenever possible. Therefore, I would not even know
how to begin to structure my lectures on dogmatics much differently than I have done all along. But I had wished that, not only
by the overall arrangement, but also by the treatment of individual topics, my book would have succeeded more than it has in
guarding against the exclusive preoccupation with its systematic
form and would have again and again made the reader conscious
that dogmatic statements are derivative, whereas the inner state
of feelings if original.[12] I would have wished to construct the
work so that at every point the reader would be made aware that
the verse John 1:14 is the basic text for all dogmatics, just as
it should be for the conduct of the ministry as a whole.

Unfortunately, I have come to realize that not everyone can
be expected to grasp these connections, as simple as they are.
If a scientific spirit and religious emotion must always walk
hand in hand in theological productions, I believe that I can
attest that the one had just as much a share in the composition
of my work as the other. In order to make this claim for the book
itself, however, I must show that it has influenced both areas,
religion and science, equally, and at present I do not believe it
has. I am convinced, however, that if I had followed the other
arrangement of the book, I would have come considerably nearer to
my goal.

[The Decision Not to Reorganize the Work]

Nevertheless, I had to forgo the attempt to improve my book
by reorganizing it. I was restrained by two reasons, which held
me back as though by an invincible power. Since one is only a
whim and the other concerns my own inability, I consoled myself
with the thought that sooner or later someone will come who will
be in a far more advantageous position to bring the project to a
happy and successful conclusion.

The whim, my friend, is my strong dislike for such an anti-
climax. If the divine wisdom and love meant no more to me than to

a pantheistic dogmatician, to use that term pejoratively as it is
used against me and others, then it would not have been possible
for me to have given them their present position, since I would
have taken care not to present my best at the outset. If I had
chosen the other arrangement of the book, which is after all not
pantheistic, then I would have concluded the book with the
natural attributes of God. Although it is true that even these
could have been treated differently than I have done, the only way
to lessen the objections would have been to shorten my account
considerably.

    After a complete discussion of the doctrines of redemption
and the kingdom of God, there would have been scarcely any other
option than to deal as briefly as possible with all those doctrines
now contained in the first part. And there can be no doubt that
this would have been detrimental not only to the book itself, nor
just as it pertains to me personally, i.e., as a reflection of my
point of view, but also as it relates to the present needs of our
church. I would not be convinced that I had done justice to my
calling if I had eliminated anything significant in this part.
You must prepare yourself for a difficult and perhaps lengthy
confession of my heart, but I cannot spare you from it.

                [Challenges Posed by Natural Science]

    Just think of the present state of the natural sciences as
they increasingly develop into a comprehensive knowledge of the
world. A short time ago no one could have conceived of this
development. What then do you suppose the future holds, not only
for our theology, but for our evangelical Christianity? I speak
here of our evangelical Christianity, for a Romish Christianity
is always available. There are those who can hack away at
science with a sword, fence themselves in with weapons at hand to
withstand the assaults of sound research and behind this fence
establish as binding a church doctrine that appears to everyone
outside as an unreal ghost to which they must pay homage if they
want to receive a proper burial. Those persons might not allow
themselves to be disturbed by the developments in the realm of
science. But we cannot do that and do not want that. Therefore,
we must make do with history as it develops.

    For this reason, I can only anticipate that we must learn to
do without what many are still accustomed to regard as inseparably
bound to the essence of Christianity. I am not referring to the
six-day creation, but to the concept of creation itself, as it is

usually understood, apart from any reference to the Mosaic chrono-
logy and despite all those rather precarious rationalizations that
interpreters have devised. How long will the concept of creation
hold out against the power of a world view constructed from un-
deniable scientific conclusions that no one can avoid, especially
now, when the secrets of the experts concern only the method and
detail of the sciences, but their great results will soon be
accessible to every enlightened and knowledgeable person throughout the general public.

As for the miracles in the New Testament (I do not want to
discuss those in the Old Testament first), it will not be long
before they will fall once more. When they do, however, it will
be for far more worthy and well-founded reasons than in the days
of the shallow *Encyclopédie*.[13] A dilemma will arise. On the one
hand, the entire story of which the miracles are a part can be
dismissed as a fable, for we are unable to determine how much historical fact underlies the entire account. Consequently, the result would be that Christianity would appear to others as having
arisen out of nothing rather than from the being of God. On the
other hand, even if we do find the stories to be historically
accurate, we will have to admit that, since they took place in
nature, it is proper to seek for analogous occurrences in nature.

Thus, the conception of miracle will not be able to continue
in its traditional form. What will happen, then, my dear friend?
I will not live to see that day, but can peacefully lay down to
sleep. But you, my friend, and your contemporaries, so many of
whom have views similar to ours, what do you plan to do? Do you
nevertheless intend to barricade yourself behind such fortifica-
tions and cut yourselves off from science? The barrage of
ridicule to which you will be subject from time to time causes
me no concern, for it will do you little harm once you are re-
signed to it. But the blockade! The complete starvation from
all science, which will follow when, because you have repudiated
it, science will be forced to display the flag of unbelief!
Shall the tangle of history so unravel that Christianity becomes
identified with barbarism and science with unbelief? To be sure,
many will make it so. Preparations are already well underway,
and already the ground heaves under our feet, as those gloomy
creatures who regard as satanic all research beyond the confines
of ancient literalism seek to creep forth from their religious
enclaves. These cannot, however, be destined to be the guardians
of the Holy Sepulcher. Nor can I imagine counting you and our
circle of friends, their students and successors, among them.

As long as this controversy between free, independent scientific
inquiry and our doctrine of faith remains unsettled, should I not
offer, or better, point out a few alternatives, for they are already
available?

[Christology in Light of the Modern World View]

Try to see if you can dismiss what has been until now essential to Christianity: belief in a divine revelation in the person
of Jesus from whom everyone can and should derive a new, powerful
heavenly life. See if you can dispense with that Jesus who for
some time now has been so honorably regarded, sometimes as the
wise man of Nazareth, and sometimes as a simple country rabbi, and
indeed as the founder of the new synagogue that so miraculously,
almost unintentionally, expanded into the Christian church, and
who tolerated its central tent, faith in himself--a belief based
on nothing but phantasies produced by trick mirrors. Yet for his
day he said some beautiful things, which we can use as mottos to
introduce our own wholesome and noble thoughts. Do you want to
limit your belief in him to the resolve to honor him for a while
longer, since it is always hazardous to shift to a new central
figure and a new book of sayings? Do you want to proceed with
the business of public education and morality along these lines?
If so, then when that future day arrives, you will have even more
excuse than at present. Such a redirection is already beginning
to be made easy from a historical perspective. Or are not the
Ebionites already highly enough praised as the authentic Christians
who fortunately kept their distance from the sentimental mysticism
of John and dialectical mysticism of Paul?[14]

There is still one other alternative. Although its historical
viewpoint is not far from the Ebionite view, it is placed on such
a more exalted and superior prospect that with its higher consciousness it can gaze down on the Ebionitic path as upon a previous highway. It is on this road, dear friend, that I am said to
have been seen. But that was only my phantom, my *Doppelgänger*.
I am referring to speculative theology. The sublime propositions
it advances, that the divine and human natures are not at all
separate, that the divine nature is the truth of human nature and
that human nature is the reality of the divine, are related to the
fundamentals of the Ebionitic view as philosophical profundity is
to the proverbial cleverness of ordinary life.

When I read that this unity of God with man is manifest and
real as an actuality in the person of Jesus, I think that it can
be a beautiful and true expression of our faith. But when I read

that the certitude of this truth is vested in the concept of the
idea of God and man, or in knowledge, then, with all due respect
to the profundity of this speculation, I must reiterate that I
cannot acknowledge that this truth grounds the certainty of my
faith. Thus, if the first two propositions do in fact represent
my philosophy (something I do not at all concede), then the third
proposition would be at best a formula expressing how this philosophy tallies with faith. But I could never confess that my faith
in Christ is derived from knowledge or philosophy, be it this
philosophy or any other.

[The Eternal Covenant]

When I think about the impending crisis, I realize that,
unless I were to exclude all science from my life, I would have
to choose between two alternatives. I can throw the origin of
Christianity in with the infinite accumulation of experience and
present it as raw material for science, which will then decide
whether it is right and worth the trouble to lift out especially
this item from the mass. Or I can take my faith on loan from
speculation, which may safeguard it from natural science, but
which will likewise set the rules and subject it to its general
constructions. Given these two alternatives, I would truly not
know which I wanted to select. For myself alone, I would
promptly choose the latter, although I fear my sense of joy
would be dulled if I were called upon to explain in detail how the
truth of the absolute filiation of God in the person of Jesus
finds its certitude in knowledge. Moreover, I suspect that
there would not remain much more of the historical person of the
redeemer than there is in the Ebionitic view. If I think of myself as a member of the church, however, and especially as a
teacher, then I must decisively reject this alternative and go
over to the opposition. The concept of the idea of God and man is
indeed a precious gem, but only a few can possess it, and I do
not want to be such a privileged person in the community that I
alone among thousands posses the ground of faith. In the community, I can exist only in complete equality, in the consciousness
that all of us draw in the same way upon this one source and have
in him the same thing. As a spokesman and teacher in the community, I would find it impossible to attempt to impart the concept
of the idea of God and man without distinguishing between young
and old. Further, with respect to our common situation, an
insurmountable barrier would separate me from the others. I would

have to regard their faith as groundless, and so I would want to
strengthen and secure it.

In short, speculative theology threatens to violate one of
Christ's statements to the effect that all should be taught of
God without any distinction between esoteric and exoteric doctrine. Only those with knowledge possess the ground of faith;
those without knowledge have only the faith itself, and therefore
they receive it only by way of tradition. Even though the
Ebionitic position leaves very little of Christ, at least the
little it leaves is equally accessible to and attainable by all.
We are thereby protected from a hierarchy of speculation with its
overtones of Romanism.

Neither the one approach nor the other is our way. Unless
the Reformation from which our church first emerged endeavors to
establish an eternal covenant between the living Christian faith
and completely free, independent scientific inquiry, so that faith
does not hinder science and science does not exclude faith, it
fails to meet adequately the needs of our time and we need another
one, no matter what it takes to establish it. Yet it is my firm
conviction that the basis for such a covenant was already established in the Reformation. It is necessary only that we become
more precisely aware of the task at hand so that we can resolve
it. This awareness is not lacking, for each of us is sufficiently
warned and doubly challenged to contribute to the resolution,
that is, to participate actively in the building up of both the
church and science.

Precisely this position, my dear friend, represents that of
my *Glaubenslehre*. Since I am firmly convinced of it, I thought I
should show as best I could that every dogma that truly represents
an element of our Christian consciousness can be so formulated
that it remains free from entanglements with science. I set this
task for myself especially in my treatment of the doctrines of
creation and preservation. This latter doctrine influenced in
this regard my account of miracles and even the miracle of
miracles, the appearance of the redeemer. I hope that even this
teaching has been elaborated in such a way that it will not en-
danger the faith and that science need not declare war against us.
If science must admit the possibility that even now matter is
beginning to form and to rotate in infinite space, then it must
also admit that in the realm of spiritual life there is an
appearance that we can only explain as a new creation, as the
beginning of a higher development of spiritual life. As long as
we do not need to draw boundaries between what is natural and

what is absolutely supernatural in actual reality (and I see
nothing that requires us to do so), we can also allow science the
freedom to take into its crucible all facts of interest to us and
to see what kind of analogies it discovers.

So, dear friend, you can see that the organizational plan
that I followed was the best one for my purpose, and for this reason I will not change it. You will readily concede that it would
not have been fitting for me first to have engaged in the description of what is truly Christian and then to have dealt with these
other topics as I have here. I do not want to praise my own work.
Nor do I want to claim that everyone must do as I have. You know
that I have never insisted on that. Yet I believe I can say that
whoever works on our doctrine of faith today without these considerations in mind either will leave the old untouched and so ac-
complish nothing--and when the master comes, he will find him
not keeping watch--or will lead us down one of those two questionable byways.

[Challenges Posed by Historical Science]

But we will have to deal not only with the natural sciences
and knowledge of the world. Historical research and criticism,
both indispensable to our field, also threaten us with the same
danger. Do you know already what the final verdict will be about
the Pentateuch and the Old Testament canon? Do you hope that the
traditional views of the messianic prophecies and even of the
prototypes will be found credible by those who have come to a
sould and lively view of historical matters? If I correctly read
the signs of the times, I cannot believe it. Some of our theologians, the respected Steudel at the forefront, do honestly believe
just that, but I fear that little will be accomplished by his fine
distinctions.[15]

Even our friend Sack, who has devoted so much space in his
Apologetik to this topic and has studied it with such love and
dedication, will not, I fear, have worked on it long enough.[16]
The belief in a special inspiration or revelation of God that con-
tinued up to a certain point of time in the Jewish nation is one
that contemporary studies of Jewish history do little to corrobor-
ate. Nor do I not think it very likely that the results of these
studies will lend that belief much more support. Consequently,
it seems to me to be essential that I state as clearly as possible
my view and strong feeling that faith in God's revelation in
Christ is not dependent upon such belief. If our doctrine of
faith were a collection or system of decisions about all the true

or alleged facts of revelation, then of course a decision would
have to be made about this point, too. But, since it is only an
account of the Christian faith as such, we ought not place this
additional burden on ourselves. The need must always arise from
within, and we do not need a prophetic plea for that. I believe that the one who would have allowed himself to be led to a
correct answer to the question "where I am to go?" by the study
of the Old Testament prophecies is still to come.

Indeed, I want to say more than, as far as I remember, is said
anywhere in my *Glaubenslehre*: a definite suspicion that those
prophecies do not fit Jesus would not even have held back from
faith a Jew of those times who would have been on the road to
belief.[17] This conviction that living Christianity and its progress do not need any support from Judaism in as old as my religious
consciousness itself. I cannot regard the attempt to prove Christ
from prophecies as a joyful task, and I regret that so many
prominent scholars still bother with it. For this reason I cannot
help but suspect that such an attempt is basically wrong and that
placing great value on these external proofs is due at least to a
lack of trust in the inner power of Christianity.

Often, however, this theory is merely symptomatic of an overall dependence on the imperfect nature and hollow elements of the
old covenant which we, who possess the more perfect covenant,
should readily give up. Moreover, I do not believe that it will
help us much in this imminent crisis. I at least do not think
it is completely true to say, as our friend Sack does in his
Apologetik, that even today the prophetic word is an inexhaus-
tible source of edification and knowledge for the Christian who
stands firm in the faith.[18] I am afraid that, the more we cling
to the old covenant and neglect to mine the riches of the new, the
wider the gap between piety and science will grow. Therefore, I
felt obliged to state quite candidly not only my assessment of
the value of the prophecies for faith, but also my views on the
relationship between Old Testament revelation and that in Christ,
and, because of its relation to these issues, on the unity of the
Old Testament and New Testament church.

And, to take up this issue immediately, the question can be
raised: how will criticism affect our view of the New Testament
canon? You do not want to restrain criticism any more than I do.
Who would not be happy to see the previously scattered comments
about the character of the Gospel of John presented in the proper
form of a critical hypothesis? Indeed, this seems inevitable.[19]
And how long do you think it will be before Dr. Schulz's view of

Matthew, though stated much too briefly, gains general acceptance,
especially since its further elaboration will make it far more
convincing?[20] And should we not also come back to the doubt that
earlier prevailed in the church about several of the epistles?
We would not lose anything essential: Christ remains the same and
our faith in him remains the same. But as for our doctrine of the
canon and of inspiration as a special activity of the Spirit pro-
ducing the canon, we must take care not to make any claims that
conflict with the universally recognized results of historical research. It will become increasingly difficult to adhere to the
principle that everything in Scripture is divine teaching, and so
it will be hard to determine which texts are Holy Scriptures and
what distinguishes them from all others.

This topic, however, could lead me even farther from the subject at hand. I wanted only to point out how my view as well as
my treatment of the doctrine of Scripture (which to my astonish-
ment has not been more vigorously attacked and indicted for approx-
imating Catholicism and has not even softened Delbrück's heart a
little toward me) is based on the same principle that the
Glaubenslehre should not be constructed as though its chief task
were to receive and hand on in a continuous tradition as much of
the previous material as possible.[21] Instead, in times such as
these our primary concern should be to take into account what
appears to me to be the inevitable and immediate future. To be
sure, we ought not to sacrifice or even obscure anything essential
to evangelical Christianity. But we must in good time rid ourselves of everything that is obviously only secondary and based on
presuppositions that are no longer valid, so that we might avoid
becoming ensnared in useless controversies that might lead many
easily to give up hope of ever grasping what is essential. As you
can see, this point is not so directly dependent on my whim as was
the first. In this regard, I will say only that, even if I had
begun the book with what is now the second part, I would have had
to treat at the outset the doctrine of Scripture, and the proper
ground of faith.

I hope that, all things considered, you will not find my whim
completely objectionable, but will praise me for having successful-
ly pursued it. But, due to my lack of ability, I fear I will
have a hard battle to fight with you. I wanted very much to ac-
complish something with my *Glaubenslehre*, but I have been only
moderately successful, and I am afraid that, if I had chosen the
other organization for my book, I would have had even less success.
My fear is not that you would judge me harshly because I was

unable to do what I had wanted, but that you might very much dis-
approve of what I wanted to do and so dismiss me with the cheap
consolation that my lack of success is only a just and inevitable
punishment for my evil intentions. To say the least, I am uncertain what your judgment on this matter is, for we have not discussed the subject in a long time.

[Defining Christianity to Permit the Inclusion of Rationalists in the Church]

I do not fear we would disagree that it is neither Christian
nor beneficial to expel the so-called rationalists from our
church community, even if it were done amiably and without ran-
cor.[22] It is painful to see how people who are basically kind
and honorable can so misjudge the true interest of the church that
they become embroiled in such a war of aggression. When a one-
sided tendency becomes as strong as it has in this case, it is my
custom--or should I say my bad habit?--to shift my weight, for what
it is worth, to the other side, lest the little boat in which we
all travel should capsize. It is not enough, then, for me to say
that I am willing to allow these worthy people called "rationalists" to remain in our church. I want also to show that they have
every right to be in the church and to remain there. My attempt
to define and to limit the concept of heresy, and to distinguish
between heresy and heterodoxy--a subject that is usually almost
competely neglected, as though the now obsolete investigations
into the fundamental articles had settled the matter--and much
else that I have stated elsewhere were directed to this goal.[23]

In contrast to the contending parties, who attempt from their
own perspectives to restrict the area of orthodoxy more and more
so that the real danger arises of dividing the church, I am inter-
ested in extending it. My intention was to demonstrate in as much
detail as possible at every key point how much distance there is
between the theses of the church and those of heresy and that within this open area how much friendly agreement is still possible
on points common to both the heterodox and orthodox. The more we
stick to this position, the easier it will be to ascertain how
much actual controversy there is about this conviction, which in
my opinion both sides are prone to attach too hastily.

I have not been as successful as I had wished, and it is now
clear to me that my mistake was made in the Introduction to my
book. Already there, where the sole concern was to show what is
characteristic of Christianity, I have defined the concept of

redemption much more narrowly than was necessary, with the result
that only the stricter view was left.[24] The Heidelberg Catechism,
which takes as its starting point the basic Christian feeling,
held me too firmly in the grips of its Fifteenth Question and what
follows.[25] Yet, I almost hesitate to say this, since it is because of this section, especially, that I have been accused of
dealing only with an ideal Christ. It may be that in the end the
good Catechism, too, because of its constructive question: "What
sort of mediator and redeemer must we then seek?" will have to be
considered gnostic.

But I am now convinced that, even if I had been fortunate
enough to avoid this snag in the Introduction--and I will have to
do so in my second edition--I would have still fallen into the
same error even if my treatment had begun with this central point.
Therefore, although I am leaving the organization unchanged in the
second edition of the book, I hope that I can come somewhat closer
to my goal in this respect.

[The Nature of Dogmatic Systemization]

Perhaps you smile as I unburden my heart and thereby willingly
fall into the trap set by my critics and so-called opponents.
However, it does seem strange that some of my critics claim that
the one merit due my work is for its systematic arrangement, when
I do not care whether or not the second part comes first. But so
be it. Of course, I do not care for poems, whether Greek or German, that can be arbitrarily begun at any line and read either
forwards or backwards.[26] Nor would I consider it feasible in
philosophical systems to reorganize the various propositions and
their groupings, if I may give my opinion as a dilettante. But a
dogmatics can never become a poem, even though its author may consider it to be no more true than poetry. Nor should it be a philosophical system, even if its author is quite philosophical. Therefore, not only is a dogmatics a quite different case, but I could
be so bold as to claim that it is advantageous for a dogmatics to
undergo such a reorganization. It is a sign that the dogmatics
stays within its limits and seeks to be nothing more than a suitable and skillful arrangement of what is simultaneously present
and mutually interrelated. The completeness of the arrangement is
proved by the arrangement itself. As long as the readers strike
the correct point, it will not matter whether they move first in
one direction or in the other. And, in truth, I would prefer to
forfeit the acclaim [for skillful organization] than to be

regarded as wanting to perform the clever trick of deducing
Christianity from anything! It would certainly be the first time
that one achieved something against one's own will. Is there any
phrase which expresses less what is essential to my work than that
I deduce Christianity from the feeling of dependence?[27] Words
are, of course, used arbitrarily, but it would have to be said at
least that I deduce all religions from this feeling. And, if one
wants to continue using language in this way, one would have to say
that I deduce Christianity from the feeling of the need for redemption, which is indeed a particular form of the feeling of dependence.

Will one also speak in terms of "deducing," however, when I
say that it was due to the liveliness of this feeling that Christianity arose when Christ appeared and was recognized in his
Lordship and power? Equally unsuitable is Tzschirner's terminology,
that is, his reference to the aesthetic principle by which I am
to my complete surprise associated with Chateaubriand and by which
the two of us are associated with Schelling, no doubt to his surprise as well.[28] My systematic skill, if I can boast of any in
dogmatics, does not depend on principles and deductions in this
sense. It is quite simply the skill of discovering an organizational plan that can convince the readers that the presentation
is complete and can refer them, if not immediately, at least by
mediation, from each dogmatic proposition back to the immediate
self-consciousness that it represents. Those who look for more
and then do not find anything should not seek recourse from me,
but to one of my all too charitable opponents.

[The Three Forms of Dogmatic Propositions]

Do not be astonished, dear friend, that I add such an epilogue
about this topic, for it is also a preface. I have seriously
debated whether there was still time for me to revise in another
way the form of my book for this second edition. I am referring
here to that revision already hinted at and, as it were, promised
in the book itself when the two forms of dogmatic propositions,
those expressing the attributes of God and those expressing the
characteristics of the world, were called derivative forms.[29]
If it is true that they do not express anything that is not in its
essential content already contained in the basic propositional
form, they could be dispensed with altogether. This is indeed my
conviction, and tied to it is the conviction that our doctrine of
faith will eventually learn to manage without them. When one has
advanced in one's career even as far as I have, is it not natural

that, once one perceived clearly how the final, completed form of
one's work must look, one tries to give it that form as soon as
possible? Upon further reflection, however, I decided that such
an undertaking would be egotistical, for too much haste would
have a harmful effect on the work itself. Indeed, the very reasons that prevented me from this approach at the start would have
kept the thought from arising again if I had not been tempted by
the polemics directed against me.

For example, Professor Baur has argued that my view of the
relationship among these three forms provides strong evidence for
what he terms my gnosticism, that is, that I deal only with an
ideal Christ and that the historical Christ means little or nothing to me.[30] I would welcome your opinion as to how much or how
little I am to blame for this misunderstanding. Ostensibly, at
least, it rests only on the statement made in my introduction to
these forms that, although the latter two forms are strictly
speaking superfluous, a system which omitted them would lack a
proper historical position and so its ecclesiastical character.[31]
Of course, these two statements are vague and obscure when they
are read out of their proper context. But is not the latter sentence clarified by the statement that immediately follows about
the differences between a dogmatics that sets forth public doctrines and a system that, although also of the spirit, sets
forth the private convictions of Christians?[32] Was it too much
to expect from attentive readers that here, where I lay out the
schematic framework of the dogmatics, they should recall the more
precise definitions of what belongs to dogmatics? Is not the term
"historical position" made clear by its immediate context and by
the preceding statement that all Christian doctrines of faith include propositions of all three forms?[33]

And if my work is a system, does not its cohesion make clear
beyond all doubt that the reference here is not to the Christian
doctrine of faith in general but to only one possible arrangement
of it? Am I in any way to blame for the confusion between the
historical position of a book and the historical character of the
Christian doctrine of faith itself? Is it my fault that the
Program translates "historical position" by the term *fundamentum
historicum* and then concludes that, if the *Glaubenslehre* would be
complete without propositions of these two derivative forms, it
would be complete without its historical fundament, i.e., the historical Christ?[34] This argument completely ignores my assertion
that these two derivative forms cannot contain anything that was
not already present in the primary form. Where do other doctrines

of faith place the historical Christ so that it would not be
necessary for mine to have a place for him as well?

Of course, you have certainly already exonerated me of this
almost inconceivable misunderstanding. Yet, since this accusation
appears to be made by everyone in the Tübingen School, you will
forgive me for not rushing to refute it by showing that, even if
all the propositions of faith were given in the first form alone,
the place of the historical Christ would be as secure and as certain as ever.[35] Without doubt it would give me no small satisfac-
tion to present the dogmatics in the distinctive form I envision
for it, free from all other materials.

Like Professor Baur, Dr. Röhr provokes me into revising my
work in this way. He contends that in my exposition I gave the
two derivative forms far more significance than I had claimed
for them.[36] Behind this complaint there seems to lurk the suspicion that, although I had declared these derivative forms to be
dispensable, I could not have presented many doctrines at all, or
at least not properly, without them. Although his voice is to be
heeded, it did not cause me to rush to make the revision, for I
come back to what I have already said: it is still far too early.
Moreover, in revising the book, I would run the danger that in this
form it would become merely a private work, as it were, a cabinet
piece of theological literature. Many would find it edifying and
instructive, but it could not have any influence on the public
proclamation of Christian doctrines because it would lack the
proper point of contact for that purpose. As a result, much of
what I had hoped to achieve would become unattainable.

Furthermore, there are a large number of dogmatic expressions
in the second and third forms to which I most vigorously object.
Therefore, I believe it is necessary that the time being I carry
on my polemic in the same form. Only a dialectical polemic, that
is, one proceeding from what is already given and examining what
is confessed, can demonstrate that it leaves the Christian faith-
content of the propositions unshaken and can insure that it will
not enslave us to some other philosophical system.[37] The guarantee and proof of its success will by necessity be in the complete
exposition of the first form by itself. Only such an exposition
will help rid us of all that scholastic rubbish still cluttering
our discipline, and we cannot be freed from that soon enough.

The method of mere simplification that has been practiced for
some time will not prove effective in the long run. The two groups
that we are speaking of here will not be satisfied by replacing
well-defined and clearly differentiated representations with vague

and imprecise ones. The scientific spirit will not view this as
progress, but as a sign of weariness with the subject. The sense
of piety, as much as it wants to get rid of sterile literalism,
would soon realize that such formulations do not arise from its
need to express itself. If this need is met by expressions of
faith stated in the basic form, that is, expressions referring
back to the immediate self-consciousness of the Christian, then
science can draw forth whatever is correct about formulations
belonging to ages long past.

This battle will not be over very soon. Therefore, in order
to write the best dogmatics possible, I must remain true to the
earlier, more complicated method and leave what I had wanted to
do myself to someone in the remote future. If I had treated all
of the doctrines according to the basic form alone and on that
basis tried to carry out my antischolastic polemics, the exposition
would have remained the same as it is now. But, inasmuch as the
propositions would no longer be coordinated, the subdivisions would
have to be multiplied, and as a result the materials would become
less manageable and the book would have become much more difficult
to comprehend. Nothing would thereby be gained. The best I can
do, then, is to retouch here and there certain details and to point
out more strongly and clearly those simpler expressions which we
should retain once the scholastic element has been eliminated.

It is just as well if nothing else is done. I have the pleasure of believing that I have glimpsed, at least from afar, a
freer and more lively way of handling our doctrine of faith. And,
thank God, I also see the way to this goal, as I have just indicated it, and I hope for the best from the scientific spirit of
the coming generation to keep our field free from forms of philosophy that may once again approach scholasticism. I also hope the
best for the sense of freedom in the piety of this coming generation. For no matter how much there may again arise the inclination to submit to the yoke of a human literalism, this sense of
freedom will certainly secure our field against all attacks of
speculation.

[Stylistic Revisions]

So, my dear friend, since I could not dare to make such major
revisions of my work, what was left for me to do in my new edition?
I have principally attempted two things. Unfortunately, I can be
certain only that one will succeed; the other I will attempt, but
I do not know with what success. Let me begin with the second

point, i.e., to shorten my work as much as possible. Whenever I
look at my book I am startled to see how it has swollen under my
hands to such a size, without my noting or willing it. It is almost as though I had suddenly changed my mind and, instead of
writing too concisely, as I am sometimes criticized for, I became
verbose. When I compare my book with similar texts that are of far
less bulk, I find that they contain an abundant treasury of recent
literature and that they give full consideration to the various
opinions expressed by distinguished scholars. How, then, can I
help but feel ashamed for consuming far more space for far less,
since I made no use of such ingredients? Therefore, I would like
to condense the book as much as possible.

There are only two limits placed upon me which I do not believe I can transgress without disadvantage. At the very least,
the book must be as understandable by itself as it is now. This
should give you little cause to smile, for I am serious. I mean
only that it ought not be necessary for the reader to refer to
some other work, my own or someone else's, in order to understand
what is said. Naturally, I exclude here my *Encyclopedia,* but only
with respect to the introductory materials.[38] I would have to
appeal to this in any theological textbook I wrote. Beyond that,
even when there is a strict correlation between them, the restric-
tion stands: all of an author's writings are to be viewed as a
whole, and each work is only a single bud on the branch of literature to which it belongs. This is an excellent rule for readers,
especially those who want to progress until they can understand
authors better than they understood themselves. The author, however, must present the "whole" in as self-contained a form as
possible. But, unless the entire discussion is to be revised, it
must still be possible to distinguish, even by the language itself,
the exposition of the propositions from the propositions themselves. Independently of its connection to our academic lectures,
this style of writing has certain advantages if it is used consis-
tently. But then each proposition is as aphoristic as possible
and makes a clear point. Nothing seems to me more strange than
when in such a book a proposition is so extensive that it can be
distinguished from its exposition only by the size of the printing
and the paragraph that follows is then titled "continuation." If,
in contrast to this practice, I were not to write the expositions
as aphoristically as the propositions, I am not sure how significant
my economizing will be. If in this attempt I am not very successful, I ask you especially to accept my good intentions in lieu of

the deed itself, for you know very well how to shift from free-
flowing to a more compressed style in the same book.[39]

If I am as successful as I would wish, a great deal of space
would be saved, for on these two points I will not deviate from
my present treatment. As for the question of so-called bibliographical literature, I would like you to consider my recommenda-
tion that it should not be included, as it now customarily is, in
books designed for use in our courses in the university. Not only
must we always take care that there is enough room to shelve these
printed pages, but in my opinion it is important that our students
have books that they can carry around comfortably. If we survey
our theological texts as a whole, we will find that all too often
they cite the same books. And if the references are written out
in full, how much room is taken up! If they are just listed, how
many of the readers will look up the passages that are cited,
especially in the newer books about which I am primarily speaking?
Therefore, I suggest this: if the teacher cannot presume that
the students have been familiarized in special preparatory lectures
with the theological works of the discipline or that they have
been made aware of the significant recent publications through survey books, or critical review notices, or by word of mouth, then
the author should include in the textbook a list of recommended
books dealing with the subject as a whole or with certain important sections, where one writer or the other offers a significant
contribution. It is not necessary, however, to refer to specific
passages. I thought I could proceed on the basis of this assumption, especially since nearly every textbook, particularly the most
popular ones, contain a host of such references. Moreover, in our
universities there is a great deal of oral tradition about both
the teachers and the texts, and it seems to have quite an influence
on our beginning students. I trust, then, that our learned contemporaries will forgive me for not adorning my book with more frequent
references to their names.

In quoting from older texts, especially patristic works, I
followed the rule that for statements that are not creedal in the
strict sense--in this case it would suffice to refer only to the
Confessions themselves--I would refer to the oldest sources I know
of, whenever they are in the form I recommend. Moreover, I held
to this resolution so firmly that I limited my references to texts
and sections where the topic in question is handled *ex professo*.
From these, I selected only the most telling and unambiguous
passages. In all honesty, then, the last thing that I expected
was Delbrück's criticism that passages torn from their contexts

do not prove much.[40] I wish he had looked up one or two passages as a test case and so tried to turn this insinuation into a
specific criticism. At any rate I live with the good hope that no
specialist will step forward in his defense. Indeed, he himself
has already compensated me adequately for his criticism on page
140 of his work.[41]

Of course, it would have been possible to discuss the complex
secondary literature, especially the new works, by using the space
I had saved to expand each article. But in my opinion a textbook
that deals with Christian faith as a whole has enough to do if it
fulfills the essential duty of defining the limits within which a
representation can move without losing its relation to the principles of the church. Moreover, since it should be possible to
gain an overview of the work without too much difficulty, the
individual articles should not be expanded in such detail that they
can no longer be distinguished from monographs. Therefore, I want
to dispense with expansions of this sort in the second edition,
and I will be satisfied if everything is placed in its proper
light.

[Changes To Be Made in the Introduction]

The other goal I have in mind is to revise the Introduction,
and this might result in certain significant changes. I cannot
disclaim all responsibility for the special attention that most of
the critics gave to the Introduction. A host of significant
misunderstandings has arisen because the critics thought of the
Introduction too much as one with the dogmatics itself. Let me
single out for you a few examples.

In the well-known *Tübingen Easter Program* it is claimed that
I try to explain Christian piety on the basis of a universal human
consciousness of piety.[42] If this remark means only that, as Baur
stated it in his review of that *Program* in the *Tübinger Zeitschrift*,
I try to specify the distinctive place Christianity occupies among
the various possible modifications of that common consciousness,
then there is no misunderstanding.[43] But the view increasingly
emerges that I wanted, as it is usually put, to demonstrate Christianity a priori. I do not see how Baur could make such a claim
unless he had sought far more in the propositions of the Introduc-
tion--the only part of the book he dealt with--than simply the
specification of the place of Christianity.

The following example makes this even clearer to me. On the
basis of my treatment of redemption in the Introduction, Baur feels
justified in concluding that for me the concept of the redeemer

is not historically given at all, but rather coincides with the
concept of redemption. Therefore, my Christianity is not based
essentially on historical fact, but is founded solely on a concept.
He says that, although I set forth the proposition that everything should be related to the consciousness of redemption in the
person of Jesus of Nazareth, in the exposition of the theses I
make no further mention of this person. Instead, I only specify
more precisely the concept of the redeemer. If Dr. Baur had kept
to the view that my concern at that point was to specify that place
of Christianity, he would have interpreted this section quite
differently, especially since he is not unfamiliar with my
Speeches on Religion.[44] All further exposition of the person of
Jesus belongs, of course, in the dogmatics because everything in
Christianity is related to this person. In the Introduction I
sought only to show how the concept of redemption, whether accomplished by this person or someone else, must be conceived if it
is to form the center of a particular type of faith.[45] Thus, when
Baur demands that the Introduction discuss the person of Christ,
he has insufficiently distinguished between the intent of the
Introduction and that of dogmatics.

His failure to distinguish the two comes to the fore most
strongly and unmistakeably when he wonders why I failed to present
the propositions in the Introduction in all three forms.[46] Indeed, to a certain extent he even demands that they should have
been so presented because only then would the real intent of my
dogmatics become manifest. But why? I speak of these three forms
only in reference to truly dogmatic propositions, and the Introduction does not contain even a single one of these. How would I
have been able to make my meaning clear if I had so confused matters that a host of other problems would have had to arise?
Everything that Baur says from his perspective and the connection
he makes, not between the three dogmatic forms to which I had
actually referred, but between the two main forms of religion on
the one side, and heathenism, Judaism, Christianity on the other
side, simply confuse the issue. I find nothing in his statements
that could help make my meaning any more clear. How could this
penetrating analyst come to demand that the Introduction include
something that properly belongs to dogmatics alone except by somehow overlooking the difference between the two?

I cannot help you; you must be patient with me as I cite still
a few more examples of these men to whom I am kindly disposed. I
am greatly indebted to my dear Schwarz for the great effort he put
into his review of my *Glaubenslehre*.[47] He is due a special word

of thanks for several points he makes, especially for recognizing
that the investigations in the Introduction are only propaedeutic
and exoteric. Nonetheless, he feels compelled to state that the
attempt made in proposition §6 to specify the correct position of
Christianity within the totality of religious communities by com-
paring and contrasting it to other types of belief does not provide an adequate foundation for Christian dogmatics.[48] But how
could it have occurred to me to try to provide such a foundation
in the Introduction! I grant that the foundation for the doctrine
of faith of any religious community would require reference both
to the necessity within self-consciousness to express itself and
to the collective will which brings forth a communal expression.
In the case of a Christian doctrine of faith, the exposition is
at the same time the foundation, since everything in the Christian
doctrine of faith can be established only as the correct expression
of the Christian self-consciousness. Unless one finds the content
in one's own self-consciousness, there can be no foundation, but
only a summons for one to locate the point where one's personal
pious consciousness deviates from the collective consciousness
presented in the doctrinal system.

The Introduction, therefore, must attempt to establish a
principle for determining what is valid in all the modifications
of Christian self-consciousness and what is not present except
within that consciousness. This principle, however, does not provide anyone with a foundation. Moreover, the Introduction does not
even once seek to trace this principle back to the total Christian
consciousness because the Introduction belongs to the realm I customarily call "philosophy of religion," although others use that
term differently.[49] Consequently, the principle could be used by
any non-Christian, too, to distinguish the pious Christian emotions
and the propositions of faith expressive of them from those that
are not Christian. Therefore, should I not here assume that Sack
also has confused the task of the Introduction with that of dogmatics itself?

One more comment is to be made about our friend Sack, that is,
about his response to my treatment of the concept of revelation.[50]
He claims that I do not consider the concept of revelation as
strictly dogmatic and that, although only from his perspective, my
assertion that absolute revelation is in Christ alone has merely
a historical content which does not affect the determination of
the concept. Now I would have thought that my treatment would be
perfect for an apologist because at this point my Introduction
was moving in the area of apologetics. I believe that the Christian

apologist can say to fellow believers: "What you call 'revealed'
cannot be sufficiently distinguished from what is not revealed,
unless you are willing to affirm that much else, which you are not
accustomed to call 'revealed' at all, or only in a very vague
sense, is just as much 'revealed' after all. But since you do
believe that the concept means something, you must permit me for
my part to consider as revealed that which is so definitely distinct from everything else that it bears comparison as a second
revelation only with God's original revelation, namely, creation."
This would not be a bad summary of the matter at all, and at the
same time it would serve to make the concept dogmatically tenable.
This is precisely what I have done.

The Introduction deals first with the concept of revelation
as something common to several or to all religions, and therefore
finds the concept to be vague. It is precisely this concept which
is historical. But Sack calls it dogmatic. When applied to
Christ, however, this same concept appropriately designates the way
God is present in Christ and so in this sense it can be used dogmatically. But Sack calls this historical. The fact that I do
not find it advisable, even in dogmatics, to use the term in a
variety of formulations does not alter the situation at all. Do
I not have good cause, then, to believe that even here Sack has
not taken seriously enough the distinction between Introduction
and the work of dogmatics itself? Is it possible that these
scholars and so many others--for I have by no means reached the
end of my list of examples--could have arrived at this view without it somehow being my fault? Indeed, I have made a conscious
effort to learn who is to blame. I have not learned much, but
what I have learned leads me to make one significant change.

Perhaps it was a drawback that the Introduction began immediately with an overall definition of dogmatics.[51] The readers may
therefore suppose that once this definition is given the dogmatics
begins, and so they might not realize that the material following
the definition should have actually preceded it. Without these
elaborations that definition would be only a lifeless literalism
and without any specific content. Perhaps this misunderstanding
could have been prevented by dividing the Introduction, like the
rest of the book, into various sections. The headings might have
helped the readers orient themselves and know exactly where they
were. As it is, the thirty-five sections continue on as one without any visible internal organization, and for this reason even
many attentive readers could become confused.

Here is my plan. In the Introduction I will first give precise explanations of all the terms before I define what dogmatics
is. Moreover, I will provide headings for the smaller sections
to indicate where the propositions that precede the constitution of
the concept of dogmatics properly belong. In this way everything
that introduces and specifies the organization of the work will
be brought into close relationship to the account of dogmatics,
and the Introduction will be rounded off into a self-enclosed
whole. Whether I will be more pleased with this arrangement, I
do not know. If so, it will be because the proper task of the
Introduction will have been met: it will be immediately evident
how this particular theological discipline relates--as it must because of its scientific form--to the sciences in general. As it
is now, the readers must find this relationship for themselves.
I had hoped, of course, that my *Brief Outline* would have clarified
this point, but the readers would then have to rely more than
necessary on something other than my dogmatics itself.[52] Therefore my plans are limited to this one essential change.

[The Language of Dogmatics and Philosophy]

In addition, I have above all considered ways of improving
the language of my book. I can try to the best of my ability
(which I do not want to say much about here) to remove the difficulties in my style of writing as much as possible without becoming verbose. I can seek to eliminate from the wording of my
own formulations the non-German terms, especially those that
definitely call to mind the philosophical schools, and replace
them with German terms free of such connotations. This will be
about all that I will be able to do. The distinctive position of
my book vis-à-vis previous formulations of church doctrine will
not permit me to do any more. Indeed, too much should not be expected from a German dogmatics in this respect. The language of
dogmatic theology is not designed to be carried over into such popular forms of communication as the sermon or catechism; in fact,
it would be unwise to make this transition too easy. The necessity
of translating the terms in which representations have come to us
into other terms guarantees that they are thought through and
internalized, as we should expect of those going into ministry.
I cannot refrain, however, from saying a few words to you about
a word of warning issued by one prominent scholar.

In an essay in the new *Zeitschrift für Theologie und Philosophie*, Professor Fries agrees with the way I distinguish between

religion and philosophy. Nonetheless, he maintains that in religious doctrine every consideration is essentially philosophical and
that anyone who tries to avoid philosophy will only fall prey to
the philosophy that is passively communicated in language, which
is a mixture of the philosophical terminology of Wolff and Fichte.[53]
You might suppose that I have nothing to say about this claim
except to reject it completely, if by religious doctrine we mean
the doctrine of some particular religious community. But if we
are speaking about a speculative theology, them I am in complete
agreement, except that I would then have to object to the term
"religious doctrine."[54]

But I am especially concerned here about what he predicts for
those who do not philosophize in a religious doctrine that is
meant to be a doctrine of faith. In my opinion, the crux of the
issue seems to be that Fries refuses to acknowledge that our
discipline has a distinctive language. Instead he poses the
dilemma: the dogmatician must speak either in the language of a
philosophical school or in ordinary language. But I do not see
the matter that way.[55] From its very beginning Christianity has
proved to be a language-forming principle for both types of language. Moreover, in the language field distinctive to Christian
piety we can distinguish only different levels, with dogmatics
as the sharpest and most precise at the top. Since this linguistic
field has been formed mainly by the re-interpretation of already
available terms, certain elements of philosophical language could
have been taken over and used for the religious field. But these
elements are then cut off from their old stems and rooted in new
ground so that the strict meaning of the school is not carried
over. Sacral and juristic language are just as usable for this
purpose as philosophical language, although juristic terms can
only by applied figuratively to the relation of humans to God and
priestly language cannot be used in its original meaning. Consequently, a language arose which, like a coin, bears a double im-
print, the one side metaphorical, the other dialectical. Both
sides of the coin must be examined in order to determine its value.
Even philosophical terms must be assimilated into this basic characteristic. Every new philosophical system is naturally productive
of language in this way. If it awakens an interest beyond the
boundaries of the school, then different levels of philosophical
language come to be formed, one strictly scientific, the other
popular. And since the philosophical interest outside of the
school is influenced by various systems without becoming embroiled

in controversies as the schools do, there gradually emerges a type
of language of the sort Fries has described.

In the light of what has been said, I also believe that, considered in and of itself, there is no harm in drawing upon this
language for use in dogmatics, without leading to confusion in
the representations or unconsciously philosophizing. But I do not
believe that the dogmatic interest relates in the same ways to
every element of philosophy. Because of the subject matter, the
philosophies of Kant and Fichte cannot offer great resources.
Not even the term "radical evil" has supplanted that of "original
sin," and few of their terms remain in the terminology of Christian
ethics.[56] Instead, the philosophies of Leibnitz and Wolff, as well
as those so-called eclectic or popular philosophies influenced by
them, have maintained their position.[57] The reason for this, however, is that those philosophies themselves dogmatize very strongly. Indeed, they do so in the same sense in which I use the word,
though that fact is not recognized because dogmatic philosophy is
spoken of in contrast to critical philosophy. On the one hand,
Wolffian language remains unmistakeably connected to scholastic
language, which was nothing but a confusion of metaphysics and
dogmatics. Therefore, by borrowing from this language, we only
vindicate our own position.

On the other hand, the foremost English philosophers who
greatly influenced pre-Kantian German philosophy proceeded from
feeling as a given.[58] For this reason, one can of course question
whether their work deserves to be called "philosophy" at all in
the strict sense of the term. But even this serves to make clear
the similarity between their method and ours, and it also shows
why we could most easily incorporate the field of language formed
under their influence. Even though this mixture of elements
drawn from the languages of different, sometimes contemporaneous,
sometimes successive, schools seems to be confused and useless for
philosophy so that every new school is justified in creating a new
language of its own, it is not useless to us because we do not
philosophize. Indeed, those elements of it that we carry over into
our dogmatic language can become completely clear, when properly
treated in our field. Therefore, since I do not think that we
could return to the language of the Bible alone in order to write
a doctrine of faith designed for a school--and no one familiar
with the task believes that advisable--we may proceed confidently
along the path we have chosen. In fact, as we become at every
moment more conscious of the difference between our procedure and
that of philosophy, we become more secure in our path. My constant

endeavor is to remain aware of this difference, or rather, this
consciousness lives and always operates in me. Consequently, I
do not believe I could unconsciously fall victim to any danger.

[Response to the Treatment of Specific Doctrines]

Concerning the distinctiveness of the book's content, however,
I deeply regret how unfruitful the interval since the first appearance of the book has been for me. It is possible that I have
missed much of the literature available in journals or dissertations,
but I feel sure that one or another of my friends would have a-
lerted me to anything significant. Therefore, I must say that,
although the number of critiques published has not been insignifi-
cant, I have been disappointed by the lack of information about,
or even discussion of, my treatment of the various Christian
doctrines. Even Dr. Steudel, who was so good as to deal with my
work at length, has up to now—although I have not read the second
installment of the *Journal*—dealt only with preliminary concepts
because he still believes that the most important thing is to defend the supernatural view, which is of course his own view.
He does not regard highly enough even the well-respected Schott
because he has let it be known that he agrees with me on some
points.[59]

Do you recall the crucial question with which Dr. Steudel
opens the discussion, and how he reduced the inquiry into miracles
to an easier question?[60] Both questions have convinced me
once again how futile this controversy is. If dogmatics is supposed
to establish principles for distinguishing the natural and supernatural, then indeed it must become metaphysical and speculative.
But I consider that as exactly the same as an intervention of
clerical power' in the secular sphere. Will it really matter in
the final analysis whether the basic facts of Christianity have
come naturally or supernaturally if the faith they produce is
nothing more than a matter of assent and the revelation they offer
is no more than an instruction?

But what reason does Steudel have to doubt that I consider
Christ to be supernatural? I do not see how such a doubt could
arise if he had been convinced that I am referring to the real
Christ. If, like Professor Baur, he does not really believe I
am, I would have at least expected that he would have examined
my Christology. After all, it would be strange if my Christology
did not in some way reflect the fact that my Christ were lacking
in reality! Some traces of docetism would have to be there.

Instead of hunting for these traces, however, Dr. Steudel himself
appears to lapse into docetism when he claims that Jesus' personality was completely unaffected by his native setting.[61] That
would make Mary, who was of Jewish blood and heritage, a mere
conduit.

His ironic remark about my rejection of the concept of accomodation is really far from being a serious argument against my
Christology.[62] I consider it as one of the merits of my book that
it raises questions about such doctrines, for by answering the
questions we are led to clarify our own representation. Just as
in England the crux of the issue is whether the question of emancipation is political or religious, so here the crux of the issue is
whether our representations of angels and devils are truly
religious or only cosmological.[63] And then the question arises
whether Jesus' representations about non-religious matters were
affected by the presence of God in him as were those about religious matters. Often in such disputes no better help can be ob-
tained than from what Plato's Socrates called a vulgar argument
(*phortikon*). And so, if we cannot agree about the nature of these
representations, I would like to ask whether we are to suppose
that Jesus accepted the Copernican representation of the relationship of the earth to the sun, something obviously cosmological,
or the common one? In my opinion, no matter how the question is
answered, it is necessary to return to the distinction I made between convictions in the stricter or in the broader sense. In
this way the validity of the distinction is confirmed.

But where is all this leading me! I was going to say that
the two Tübingen theologians I named have every right to search
for any errors in my Christology that may have arisen from false
assumptions. Likewise each of my learned critics who have focused
only on my fundamental principles would have had to find the consequences of these false or unchristian principles in my treatment
of the actual doctrines themselves. If I rob religion of all
worth, if I am almost a Cyrenian, would this not necessarily be
reflected in the doctrines of the Holy Spirit and sanctification?[64]
Unfortunately, these gentlemen did not deem it worth their effort
to accompany me so far. Now, of course, I could not have expected
them to do so, especially if it were true that I often smuggle in
new ideas in the disguise of ecclesiastical terms, as a young
theologian who is beginning his career in a brilliant, almost
blinding way puts it. I think, however, that, whenever I actually
deviate from the viewpoint of the church, I criticize the church's
language as well. And, since I then go on to explain in what sense

the terminology could still be valid, I do not believe that I can
mislead an attentive reader or give a false impression of orthodoxy, which is what this insinuation amounts to.

A few hints about particular doctrines are to be found in the
comprehensive review in the journal *Hermes*.[65] Some years ago
friend promised that he would take issue with the view of
eschatology in my *Glaubenslehre*. That would have been without
doubt inspiring and instructive, but so far he has failed to keep
his word. Nitzsch led me to expect that he would express some of
his critical reservations.[66] I certainly have more to expect from
Twesten, if he continues his work, but I do wish it were already
available.[67] So I am left almost completely to myself and of
course to the comparison of my book with others. Yet I do not
want to yield to the temptation to stroll with you through the
recent literature on dogmatics and point out as we go how much or
how little I have gained from these works.

[The Relationship of Religion and Philosophy]

Let me say a few words about the various recommendations that
one friend or another gave me for my second edition. Some have
strongly urged me--and I would like to myself because the dispute
over this issue is so great--to state clearly and explicitly, and
not just with vague hints, what I think to be the relationship
between religion and philosophy (as one puts it), or between dogmatics and philosophy (as another suggests), or between the higher
self-consciousness where I begin and the original notion of God
which I apparently admit (as a third states it). But how can such
a discussion be included in a dogmatics, I mean, in mine? Both
the form and content of my *Glaubenslehre* are conditioned by the
presupposition that the notion of God set forth in it is not
original, but develops from reflection on the higher self-consciousness. I believe I have made it clear that the original
notion of God--and I must always speak of that problematically,
lest I overstep the bounds of dogmatics--would lead into the realm
of speculation. This, I believe, I have stated clearly enough,
and, if not, it can be drawn from first Explanations of my
Speeches on Religion.[68] In my opinion, the connection between
this original notion and this original self-consciousness is no
other than, and also just as much as, that between any other product of the various intellectual functions that are at the same
level and have the same relation. Consequently, I do not see how
there can be any question about how I relate religion and

philosophy. I sincerely believe and hope always to believe--and
it will be believed long after me and perhaps even more than
now--that the two can co-exist very well in the same person.
Philosophy does not need to raise itself above Christ, and, you
understand, I mean here the real, historical Christ, as though
piety were only immature philosophy and all philosophy were the
first coming to consciousness of piety. Rather, a true philosopher can be and remain a true believer, and, likewise, one can be
a pious with all one's heart and still have and exercise the
courage to delve into the very depths of speculation.

But I also know that the one can exist without the other.
Therefore, in some persons piety can come to complete consciousness even in the strictest form, that is, the form of dogmatics,
without a granule of philosophy entering into it. On the other
hand, some can empty the cup of speculation without discovering
piety at its bottom. But, since the same can be said of the relationship between piety and any number of other intellectual
activities, why should I treat just this one relation and not the
others?

As for the relationship between dogmatics and philosophy, I
must confess that I prefer to talk about it as little as possible.
Have not the philosophers complained long enough that in the
Scholastic period philosophy was both in the service of our
church's faith and under its control? Be that as it may, at least
philosophy has now become free enough. The faith that returns to
its original source no longer has any need of its service, even
for the dogmatic formulation of church doctrine. Moreover, a
church better informed of its own interest would not want to exert
any pressure on philosophy. If philosophy has since used its freedom to express its hostility to church doctrine, then it is up to
the church to look after itself, and it should be able to do so
without either attacking philosophy or courting its favor.

I am well aware that many will ask which philosophy I have in
mind. Obviously I am talking about something that does not even
exist! But my reply is that we theologians are not called upon to
adjudicate such disputes because we would not even think of po-
licing a foreign territory. Certain people claim to be philosophers, the world regards them as such, and we do, too. If it becomes established that church doctrine, when correctly presented
as the content of faith, cannot conflict with true philosophy, all
the better! But we theologians cannot attempt in any way to
guarantee that.

Therefore, if philosophy is sometimes for us and sometimes against us, we have no fixed relationship to it since the two of us have become free of each other. This is the only statement it seems advisable for me to make and to confirm in my work. To demand more makes it seem as though we should apologize to philosophy because the relationship is not different, and is what it is, as though we had to fulfill certain obligations to each other. Indeed, even if philosophy offers with the best intentions to help us come to that perfect self-understanding that it alone can give, something that I would grant it can do in every area of science, I would nevertheless say that, if we are unable to understand ourselves in our own terms, the fault must lie in something that philosophy cannot provide, so far as it presumes to be more than logic and grammar in the usual sense of those terms.

Therefore, let me stand by my *timeo Danaos et dona ferentes*.[69] I am happy that I have remained faithful to this goal and to my own philosophical dilettantism. Even if I had referred more often to the domain of philosophy, I would still follow the rule of not allowing philosophy to influence the content of the *Glaubenslehre*. Of course, how faithful I have been to my resolution is another matter, but, for the time being, the signs are fairly good. One person firmly maintains that I based my work on Jacobi and another contends it is based on Schelling, and the only proof these two can adduce are strange insertions and unwarranted suppositions.[70] Even someone as knowledgeable as our friend from Bonn can come to no other view of my way of philosophizing than that I would start out not with a feeling but with a notion and that in other respects it is about the same as the church's doctrine of faith.[71] All things considered, then, it would seem that very little of philosophy or of philosophers is to be encountered in my work. And in this matter I am far from wanting anything else. Were I to find that the content of even one proposition was speculative or could justly be considered so, I would remove this inappropriate garment from it or strike it out.

I am not thereby throwing down the gauntlet to speculative theology. On the contrary, I am willing to let it go its own way. I will let the church make use of it as it pleases. Likewise, I leave open the question whether the prevailing school will be any more successful than previous ones in legitimizing the age of scholasticism or restoring it by some means. But for my own part, I want to dissociate myself as much as possible from such attempts.

[The Conflict between Rationalism and Supernaturalism]

Some persons have focused on another, even more difficult
point and sought to make much out of what I said about the supernatural in Christian revelation and the natural development of
the divine plan of salvation. Yet many do not find in my statements sufficient basis for deciding where I stand in regard to
the controversy between rationalism and supernaturalism. To avoid
all further misunderstandings, then, I would like to make a more
satisfactory statement. These friends will hardly be pleased with
what I have just written you here. But I do not know how to comply
with their wishes, for I am convinced that misunderstandings are
unavoidable because the entire issue is a misunderstanding. I
would have thought one only needs to read the essay by Steudel--I
am acquainted only with its first part--which deals with the
attempts to reconcile the two parties, in order to be convinced
of that.[72] Even the names of the contending parties are most
unfortunate. The one refers to the nature of the event and the
other to the source of knowledge of doctrine. Why is it impossible
for persons to be convinced that certain events are supernatural
and yet to maintain that they cannot be asked to accept doctrines
that are unintelligible and cannot be rationally reconstructed?
And why is it impossible for others to say that they are inclined
to accept certain doctrines that are consoling, even though they
cannot incorporate these doctrines into the general context of the
teachings of reason, as long as these doctrines have a definite
meaning? Nonetheless, they are not prepared to form representations about facts that cannot be assimilated into the overall
fabric of experience as long as it is possible to form another
representation about them. It does not help to say that the problem does not lie in the names, but in the issue itself. If the
issue (i.e., the true nature of this great division in our church,
which I will by no means deny exists) were correctly grasped, then
suitable names would be found. Names, however, will always be
important, and what is opposed by the one group will be attributed
to the other. That is quite possible in such a complex matter because there was really no opposition. But this is no way to avoid
confusion, and why should one get into this fray unless one must?
What do you think?

Quite recently a new type of rationalism has been devised--I
would almost like to think it was done for me especially, but
that would be to give me too much honor. It seems to me that it
is called "ideal rationalism," and it refers to the belief that

something natural could at the same time be something supernatural.[73] As grateful as I am for this suggestion, I know of an
even better one. Whenever I speak of the supernatural, I do so
with reference to whatever comes first, but afterwards it becomes
secondly something natural. Thus creation is supernatural, but it
afterwards becomes the natural order. Likewise, in his origin
Christ is supernatural, but he also becomes natural, as a genuine
human being. The Holy Spirit and the Christian church can be
treated in the same way.

Therefore, I would prefer that one devise for me a position
where what is supernatural can at the same time be natural. If
the former view was called rationalism, this view would have to be
a supernaturalism, and why should it not be called real? And so
I want to say that I consider myself to be a real supernaturalist,
and I think this label is as good as any other. But I fail to see
what is to be gained from all this. And, if one is no more precise than even Professor Baur, I do not see what could prevent
someone from making into a rationalist or a supernaturalist, as
they please, one who simply does not stand at the utter extremes,
even if this person does not sing a tenth of an internal higher or
lower.

My deal friend, it is indeed time for me to stop. I do not
want to say "break off," for you need not prepare yourself for
another such desultory epistle, even though I would have liked to
dispose of various other things. But the longer here, the longer
there, and it is high time for me to begin work in earnest on my
dogmatics itself. Best wishes for yourself and your teaching.
The new semester is upon us, my fiftieth.[74] Perhaps it will bring
me one or another of your fine pupils. I am sending you one of
mine who is to give you my most friendly greetings and my assur-
ance that I remain steadfastly yours, Schleiermacher.

NOTES TO THE TRANSLATORS' INTRODUCTION

[1]Friedrich Daniel Ernst Schleiermacher, "Über seine *Glaubens-lehre* an Herrn Dr. Lücke, zwei Sendschreiben," *ThStK* 2 (1829): 255-84 and 481-532. Hereafter referred to by the short title, *The Letters to Lücke*.

[2]The reception accorded Schleiermacher's dogmatics is described by Karl Dunkmann, *Die Nachwirkungen der theologischen Prinzipienlehre Schleiermachers*, Beiträge zur Förderung christlicher Theologie, ed. D. A. Schlatter and D. W. Lütgert, Heft 2 (Gutersloh: C. Bertelsmann, 1915); Friedrich Wilhelm Gess, *Deutliche und möglichst vollständige Übersicht über das theologische System Dr. Friedrich Schleiermachers*, 2d ed. (Reutlingen: Ensslin und Laiblin, 1837); Wilhelm Herrmann, *Geschichte der protestantischen Dogmatik, von Melanchthon bis Schleiermacher*, (Leipzig: Breitkopf und Hartel, 1842), pp. 278-311; Hermann Mulert, "Die Aufnahme der *Glaubenslehre* Schleiermachers," *ZThK* 18 (1908): 107-39; idem, "Nachlese zu dem Artikel," *ZThK* 19 (1909): 243-46; and Heinrich Scholz, "Analekta zu Schleiermacher," *ZThK* 21 (1911): 293-314.

[3]See above, p. 64.

[4]*CG*, [1]§1; cf. [2]§19.

[5]Friedrich Daniel Ernst Schleiermacher, *Kurze Darstellung des theologischen Studiums zum behuf einleitender Vorlesungen*, Kritische Ausgabe, ed. Heinrich Scholz (Leipzig: A. Deichert, 1910); E. T.: *Brief Outline of the Study of Theology*, trans. William Farrer (Edinburgh: T. & T. Clark, 1850; reprint ed., Lexington, Ky.: American Theological Library Association, 1963); and *Brief Outline on the Study of Theology*, trans. from the 3d German ed. by Terrence N. Tice (Richmond, Va.: John Knox Press, 1966), §§1, 5-7, 11-12; and 25. Unless otherwise noted, all references are to the Tice edition.

[6]Ibid., §§24-31, 94-97, and 195-231.

[7]*CG*, [1]§3; [2]§15.

[8]Ibid., [2]§§16-17 bring together and revise portions of [1]§§2; 3,2; 4,1-2; and 23,1-2.

[9]Ibid., [1]§2; [2]§16.

[10]Ibid., [1]§§5-22.

[11]See above, pp. 56-58.

[12]*CG*, [2]§1. See above, pp. 56-59, 76-80.

[13]*CG*, [1]§1; [2]§19.

[14]See above, pp. 76, 78.

[15]See above, pp. 40-43.

[16]*CG*, [1]§§23-35; [2]§§20-31.

[17]Ibid., [1]§31,3 and 33; [2]§29.

[18]Ibid., [1]§§34-35; [2]§§30-31.

[19]See above, pp. 55-60.

[20]See above, p. 58.

[21]See above, pp. 69-70.

[22]*CG*, [1]§33; cf. [2]§29.

[23]See above, p. 72.

[24]*CG*, [1]§1,5; cf. [2]§19, Postscript and §16, Postscript.

[25]See above, p. 40.

[26]*CG*, [1]§9.

[27]Immanuel Kant, *Religion within the Limits of Reason Alone*, trans. Theodore M. Greene and Hoyt H. Hudson with a new essay, "The Ethical Significance of Kant's Religion," by John R. Silber (New York: Harper & Row, Harper Torchbooks, 1960), p. 173.

[28]Paul Seifert, *Die Theologie des jungen Schleiermacher*, Beiträge zur Förderung christlicher Theologie, ed. Paul Althaus, Hermann Dörries, and Joachim Jeremias, vol. 49 (Gerd Mohn: Gutersloher Verlagshaus, 1960), p. 115.

[29]Theodor Holzdeppe Jørgensen, *Das religionsphilosophische Offenbarungsverständnis des späteren Schleiermacher*, Beiträge zur historischen Theologie, ed. Gerhard Ebeling, vol. 53 (Tübingen: J. C. B. Mohr [Paul Siebeck], 1977), pp. 50-78; Volker Weymann, *Glaube als Lebensvorzug und der Lebensbezug des Denkens: Eine Untersuchung zur Glaubenslehre Friedrich Schleiermachers* (Göttingen: Vandenhoeck, 1977), pp. 26-32.

[30]Friedrich Daniel Ernst Schleiermacher, *Dialektik, Auftrag der preussichen Akademie der Wissenschaften auf Grund bisher unveröffentlichen Materials*, ed. Rudolf Odebrecht (Leipzig: J. C. Hinrichs, 1942); idem, *Schleiermachers Werke in Auswahl*, 2d ed., edited by Otto Braun and Johannes Bauer, vol. 2: *Grundlinien einer Kritik der bisherigen Sittenlehre* (Aalen: Scientia Verlag, 1967); and idem, *Psychologie. Aus Schleiermachers handschriften Nachlasse und geschriebenen Vorlesungen*, ed. L. Georg, in *SW* III, 6.

[31]Jørgensen, *Religionsphilosophischen Offenbarungsverständnis*, p. 62.

[32]Cf. *CG*, [1]§8, note a and [2]§3,2.

[33]Ibid., [1]§8; [2]§3.

[34]Ibid., [1]§8, note b; [2]§3,4.

[35]Ibid., [1]§8, note a; [2]§3,2.

[36]Ibid.

[37]Georg Friedrich Wilhelm Hegel, "Vorwort zur Hinrichs' *Religionsphilosophie*," in *Berliner Schriften: 1818-31*, ed. Johannes Hoffmeister (Hamburg: Felix Meiner, 1956).

[38]Schleiermacher an de Wette, Summer 1823, in *ASL* 4:309. "For his part Hegel continues to grumble in his lectures, as he had already published in his Preface [*Vorrede*] to Hinrich's *Religionsphilosophie*, against my animal ignorance [*thierische Unwissenheit*] about God and [he] recommends Marheinecke's theology exclusively."

[39]Cf. *CG*, [1]§9 and [2]§4.

[40]Ibid., [1]§9,3 and [2]§4,2.

[41]Ibid., [2]§4,3.

[42]Ibid.

[43]Ibid., [2]§8, Postscript 2; cf. [1]§15,5.

[44]See above, p. 46.

[45]See above, pp. 43-46.

[46]Cf. *CG*, [1]§9 and [2]§4.

[47]Ibid., [1]§9,3, Postscript.

[48]Ibid., [2]§4,4.

[49]Ibid.

[50]Ibid.

[51]Ibid.

[52]See above, p. 166.

[53]See, for example, the work of Ritschl's student, Wilhelm Bender, *Schleiermachers Theologie nach ihren philosophischen Grundlagen dargestellt* (Nördlingen: C. H. Bech'sche Buchhandlung, 1876). The Barthian perspective is evident in Felix Flückiger, *Philosophie und Theologie bei Schleiermacher* (Zurich-Zollikan: Evangelischer Verlag, A. G., 1947).

[54]See above, pp. 41-43.

[55]Carl Albrecht Bernoulli, *Die wissenschaftliche und die kirchliche Methode in der Theologie: Ein enzyklopadischer Versuch* (Freiburg, i.B.: Mohr, 1897); Hermann Süskind, *Der Einfluss Schellings auf die Entwicklung von Schleiermachers System* (Tübingen: Mohr, 1909; and Ernst Troeltsch, "Rückblick auf ein halbes Jahrhundert der theologischen Wissenschaft," *Zeitschrift für wissenschaftliche Theologie* 51 (1908): 193-226.

[56]See above, p. 86.

[57]See above, pp. 85-87.

[58]See above, pp. 81-83, 86-87.

[59]See Richard B. Brandt, *The Philosophy of Schleiermacher: The Development of his Theory of Scientific and Religious Knowledge* (New York: Harper & Brothers, 1941), esp. chap. 6.

[60]Schleiermacher, *Dialektik*, pp. 265-86.

[61]Ibid., pp. 286-97.

[62]Kant, *Religion within the Limits of Reason Alone*, pp. li-lii.

[63]Schleiermacher, *Dialektik*, p. 292.

[64]See Schleiermacher an Jacobi, 30 March 1818, in Martin Cordes, "Der Brief Schleiermachers an Jacobi," *ZThK* 68 (1970): 209-10

[65]See above, pp. 36-37, 71-72, 76-77.

[66]See above, p. 71.

[67]See above, pp. 71-72.

[68]See above, pp. 36-37, 46-47, 72.

[69]See above, p. 25; see also *CG* [1]§18 and [2]§11.

[70]*CG*, [1]§25,3; [2]§22,2.

[71]Friedrich Schleiermacher, *The Life of Jesus*, trans. S. Maclean Gilmour, ed. Jack C. Verheyden, Lives of Jesus Series, ed. Leander E. Keck (Phil.: Fortress Press, 1975) esp. pp. xlvi-lviii.

[72]*SW*, I, 2:575-653

[73]Hermann Mulert, ed., *Schleiermachers Sendschreiben über seine Glaubenslehre an Lücke*, Studien zur Geschichte des neuern Protestantismus, ed. H. Hoffmann and L. Zscharnach (Giessen: A. Töpelman, 1908).

[74]This task depends upon Carl Stange, ed., *Schleiermachers Glaubenslehre, Kritische Ausgabe--Erste Abteilung: Einleitung*, Quellenschriften zur Geschichte des Protestantismus, ed. Carl Stange, Heft 9 (Leipzig: A. Deichert'sche Verlagsbuchhandlung, 1910).

NOTES TO THE FIRST LETTER

[1]At the time this work was released, Gottfried Christian Friedrich Lücke (1791-1855) was Professor of New Testament at Göttingen. After studies at Halle and Göttingen, Lücke had enrolled at Berlin to work with Schleiermacher. From 1816 to 1818 he lectured there, developing close friendships with Schleiermacher, Wilhelm DeWette, and Johann August Wilhelm Neander. With Schleiermacher and DeWette he coedited the journal *Theologische Zeitschrift* and collaborated with DeWette on the *Synopsis Evangelorum* (Berlin: Bernoli, 1818). Before appointment to Göttingen, he was Professor of Theology at Bonn (1818-27).

Lücke was a leading representative of "mediating theology," which sought to promote two goals: first, to bridge the gap between supernaturalism and rationalism by positively combining Christian faith and modern science, and second, to provide a theological basis for the union between the Lutheran and Reformed churches in Germany. With Karl Immanuel Nitzsch, J. K. L. Gieseler, Carl Ullmann, and F. W. C. Umbreit, he founded the main organ of publication for this group, *Theologische Studien und Kritiken*, where, in the second year of its operation, these letters appeared.

At the time of the journal's establishment, Lücke had become embroiled in a controversy with Ferdinand Delbrück on the relation between the Scriptures and the rule of faith. In response to the opinions that Delbrück expressed in *Philipp Melanchthon, der Glaubenslehre: eine Streitschrift* (1826), the second volume of his major work, *Christentum: Betrachtungen und Untersuchungen*, 3 vols. (Bonn: Adolf Marcus, 1822-27), Lücke joined Nitzsch and Karl Heinrich Sack in writing *Über das Ansehen der heiligen Schrift und ihr Verhältnis zur Glaubensregel in der protestantischen und in der alten Kirche, Drei theologische Sendschreiben an Herrn Professor D. Delbrück in Beziehung auf dessen Streitschrift: "Philipp Melanchthon, der Glaubenslehrer," von D. K. H. Sack, D. C. J. Nitzsch, und D. Fr. Lücke, Nebst einer brieflichen Zugabe des Herrn D. Schleiermacher über die ihn betreffenden Stellen der Streitschrift* (Bonn: Eduard Weber, 1827).

Lücke's publications focused on hermeneutics, the canon, and the Johannine writings. His major works include the *Grundriss der neutestamentlichen Hermeneutik und ihrer Geschichte* (Göttingen: Vanderhoeck und Ruprecht, 1817); *Über den neutestamentlichen Kanon des Eusebius* (Berlin: F. Dumler, 1816), and the *Kommentar über die Schriften des Evangelisten Johannes*, 4 vols. (Berlin: Eduard Weber, 1820-22). While at Göttingen he reworked his commentary on John and published introductions to the Book of Revelation and to apocalyptic literature. His review articles appeared frequently in the *Göttingen Gelehrten Anzeigen*, where his judgments on Ferdinand Christian Baur, David Friedrich Strauss, and others received much attention. During this period he also published a series of letters to the Grimm Brothers and biographies of his teachers: Gottlieb Jakob Planck, de Wette, and Schleiermacher ("Erinnerungen an Dr. Friedrich Schleiermacher," *ThStK* 7 (1834): 745-813; E. T.: "Reminiscences of Schleiermacher," *Christian Examiner* 20 (1836): 1-46; and Schleiermacher, *Brief Outline*, trans. Farrer, pp. 1-86.

[2]The first edition of *CG* was published in 1820-21; the second edition in 1830-31.

[3]A second printing was in fact issued in Reutlingen by J. J. Mäcken in 1828.

[4]Schleiermacher to Joachim Christian Gass, 12 November 1829,
in Wilhelm Gass, ed., *Schleiermachers Briefwechsel mit Joachim
Christian Gass* (Berlin: G. Reimer, 1852), pp. 219-20: "Up until
now no paragraph has remained as it was, but I write everything
anew. The content of course remains completely the same."

[5]Christlieb Julius Braniss, *Über Schleiermachers Glaubenslehre: Ein kritischer Versuch* (Berlin: Duncker und Humblot, 1821).
The concluding sentence (p. 197), "the work in itself annuls
itself," sums up Braniss' argument that Schleiermacher's system
is fundamentally self-contradictory. On the one hand, Schleiermacher maintains that divine causality must be so understood that
historical revelation does not contradict the general nexus of
history, but can be equated with it. On the other hand, he equates
redemption with the efficacy of Jesus, who is not only the beginning but the perfection of faith. Since Schleiermacher's conception
of the absolutely sinless development of Christ cannot be
reconciled with any form of natural causality, Braniss concludes
that Schleiermacher must give up either his view of a fully sinless Christ or his view of divine causality. The affirmation of
both is the basic contradiction in the book.
      Biographical Note: Professor of Philosophy in Breslau,
Braniss (1792-1873) published mainly on logic, metaphysics, and
this history of philosophy. Next to his book on Schleiermacher,
his best known work is *Die Logik in ihren Verhältnis zur
Philosophie, geschichtlich betrachtet* (Berlin: G. Reimer, 1823).
The only full-length study is Gunter Scholtz, *'Historismus' als
spekulative Geschichtsphilosophie: Christlieb Julius Braniss
(1792-1873)* (Frankfurt: Vittorio Klostermann, 1973).

[6]Johann Friedrich Ferdinand Delbrück concluded his *Erörterungen einiger Hauptstücke in Dr. Friedrich Schleiermachers christliche Glaubenslehre* (Bonn: Adolf Marcus, 1827) by stating that
"the *Glaubenslehre* is in its innermost essence irreconcilable
with the basic principles of apostolic Christianity" (p. 190).
      Biographical Note: Delbrück (1772-1848) studied at the
University of Halle, where he received his doctorate for a study
on the religion of Homer. After teaching at a high school in
Berlin and serving as the tutor of the crown prince, he became in
1818 professor at the University of Bonn. It was during his
years at Bonn that he engaged in controversy with Schleiermacher.
His book *Philip Melanchthon: der Glaubenslehrer* led Sack, Nitzsch,
and Lucke to write *Über das Ansehen* (see n. I, 1 above). The
letter of Schleiermacher appended to that volume occasioned
Delbrück's *Erörterungen.* (see n. I, 87 below). Delbrück's response to *The Letters to Lücke* and the correspondence between
himself and Schleiermacher are printed in his book *Der verewigte
Schleiermacher* (Bonn: Adolf Marcus, 1837).

[7]Heinrich Gottlieb Tzschirner, *Briefe eines Deutschen an die
Herren Chateaubriand, de la Mannais und Montlosier über Gegenstände
der Religion und Politik*, ed. Krug (Leipzig: Johann Ambrosius
Barth, 1828), pp. 28 and 33. See also nn. I, 14 and II, 28 below.
      Biographical Note: Tzschirner (1778-1828) taught at
Wittenberg before his appointment to the faculty at Leipzig in
1809. In 1815 he added to his academic responsibilities those of
the Superintendent of Leipzig and pastor of the Thomaskirche.
One of the most influential preachers of his day, he promoted a
type of supernaturalism modified by Kantian ethics. He is best
known for his political interpretations of confessional differences: *Der Übertritt des Herrn von Haller zur katholischen Kirche*
(Leipzig: Johann Ambrosius Barth, 1821); *Protestantismus und*

Katholicismus aus dem Standpunkt der Politik (Leipzig: Johann
Ambrosius Barth, 1822); and *Sendschreiben an Abt Precht* (Leipzig:
Johann Ambrosius Barth, 1824). His own views on dogmatics were
published posthumously in *Vorlesungen über die christliche
Glaubenslehre*, ed. Karl Hase (Leipzig: Johann Ambrosius Barth,
1829).

[8]Isaaco Rust, *De nonnullis, quae in theologia nostrae aetatis
dogmatica desiderantur*(Erlangen: Kunstmann, 1828), pp. 65-69.
Rust identifies three stages in the religious-cultural development of the human race: the stage of feeling--paganism, the
stage of understanding (*intelligentia*)--Judaism, and the stage of
reason (*ratio*)--Christianity. Since Schleiermacher defines piety
as feeling, Rust believes that he re-introduces paganism into
Christianity, thereby corrupting the dignity of religion and the
essence of Christianity.

 Biographical Note: A student of Daub, Hegel, and Paulus,
Rust (1796-1862) served in several pastorates before his appointment as Professor of Theology at Erlangen in 1830. Before *De
nonnullis*, he had published *Philosophie und Christentum oder
Wissen und Glauben* (Mannheim: Schwann & Götz, 1825). From 1833
on, his career led him into administrative posts of the church,
e.g., the Consistory of Speier, the Consistory of Munich, and
the Cultural Ministry for the Pfalz. His theological position
may be termed rationalistic until the Erlangen period, after
which his writings become more orthodox.

[9]Karl Gottlieb Bretschneider evaluated the *CG* in two essays
and in an Appendix to his theological textbook. His major work,
*Handbuch der Dogmatik der evangelischen lutherischen Kirche; oder
Versuch einer beurtheilenden Darstellung der Grundsätze welche
diese Kirche in ihren symbolischen Schriften ausgesprochen hat*
(Leipzig: Johann Ambrosius Barth, 1814-18) was among the most
widely used texts of its day. The third edition of 1828 contained
an Appendix entitled "Nebst einer Abhandlung über die Grundansichten der Herren Prof. Dr. Schleiermacher und Marheinecke, sowie
über die des Herrn Dr. Hase"; cf. an excerpt from the fourth
edition, E.T.: "Bretschneider's View of the Theology of
Schleiermacher," *Bibliotheca Sacra* 10 (1853): 598-616. The
Appendix was published separately as a book in 1828 by Johann
Ambrosius Barth in Leipzig (hereafter referred to as *Grundansichten*).

 In addition, Bretschneider wrote two articles critical of
Schleiermacher: "Über das Princip der christlichen Glaubenslehre
des H. Prof. Schleiermacher: Ein Versuch," *JP* 66 (1825): 1-28;
and "Über den Begriff der Erlösung und die damit zusammenhängenden
Vorstellungen von Sünde und Erbsünde in der christliche Glaubenslehre des H. Prof. Dr. Schleiermacher," *JP* 67 (1825): 1-33.

 Schleiermacher's affinity with Roman papalism is discussed
in *Grundansichten*, pp. 65-69. This charge is based upon the
method employed by Schleiermacher and Marheinecke. Instead of
accepting the scriptures as the norm of church doctrine as the
Reformation demanded, they advance their purely philosophical
systems in the form of church dogmatics. Hence they present as
divine and indispensable much that is not contained in the Bible.
Rather than distinguishing what is based on scripture from what is
not, they employ an allegorical method to interpret all church
doctrine. According to Bretschneider, such a method can justify
every dogma, be it evangelical or Roman Catholic. It can even
support the papal system insofar as the Pope can be viewed as
symbolic of the unity of the God-consciousness present in
believers, of the developing personality of God, and of the unity
of faith. The method would also allow a Roman Catholic

understanding of the mass as a sacrifice, interpreted as symbolic
of enduring love or of the sacrifice of the self to the evolving
personality of God.

    Biographical Note: Often classified as a "rational
supernaturalist," Bretschneider (1776-1848) studied at Leipzig
and Dresden before completing his studies at Wittenberg in 1804,
where he remained to lecture from 1804 to 1807. After a year
in a pastorate (1807), he became Superintendent in Annaberge.
From 1816 until his death he was General Superintendent in Gotha.
Besides his textbook on dogmatics, his publications focused on
the Old Testament apocrypha, the Johannine literature, and the
Reformation. He helped found the *Corpus Reformatorum* and edited
Philipp Melanchthon's works for that series.

[10]In *Erörterungen,* Delbrück argues that Schleiermacher's
teaching not only advocates pantheism and denies creation but
serves to undermine moral responsibility.

[11]The epithet means "most venerable."

[12]Ferdinand Christian Baur describes Schleiermacher's *Glaubenslehre* as a form of gnosis in his inaugural dissertation, *Primae
rationalismi et supranaturalismi historiae capita potiora,* published in three parts by Hopferi de l'Orme in Tübingen: pt. 1,
De gnosticorum Christianismo ideali (1827); pt. 2, *Comparatur
gnosticismus cum Schleiermacherianae theologiae indole* (1827);
and pt. 3, *Exponitur praesertim Arianismi indoles rationali* (1828).
The charge is repeated in Baur's summary of pts. 1 and 2 of his
dissertation, "Anzeige der beiden academischen Schriften," *TZTh* 1
(1828): 220-64, as well as in his later work, *Die christliche
Gnosis, oder die christliche Religions-Philosophie in ihrer
geschichtlichen Entwicklung* (Tübingen: C. F. Osiander, 1835;
reprint ed., Darmstadt: Wissenschaftliche Buchgesellschaft, 1965),
pp. 628-68. This latter work contains a lengthy footnote (n. 22,
pp. 646-52) dealing with Baur's response to Schleiermacher's
self-defense in these letters.

    In his dissertation and its summary, Baur differentiated
two types of rationalism. There is the "ordinary rationalism"
of the Enlightenment, which is based upon the autonomy of reason,
and an "ideal rationalism," based on historical forms proper to
supernaturalism. This ideal rationalism represents those
historical forms of consciousness in which the ideas of reason
appear in the course of temporal-historical development. Baur
regards this ideal rationalism to be characteristic of gnosticism
as a Christian form of the philosophy of religion. Despite
Schleiermacher's assertions to the contrary, the *Glaubenslehre*
exemplifies ideal rationalism because it seeks to mediate between
the supernaturalism of traditional church doctrine and the claims
of reason.

    Biographical Note: Born in Wurttemberg, Baur (1792-1860)
was graduated from Tübingen University. From 1817 to 1825 he
taught history and philosophy at Blaubeuren, and in 1826 he accepted
appointment as Professor of Theology at Tübingen, where he remained until his death. Influenced by Hegel and Schleiermacher,
he is considered the leading representative of the second or "new"
Tübingen school, which applied scientific or historical-critical
methodology to the study of Christian origins, church history,
and the history of theology. See Peter C. Hodgson, *The Formation
of Historical Theology: A Study of Ferdinand Christian Baur,*
Makers of Modern Theology, ed. Jaroslav Pelikan (New York:
Harper and Row, 1966), esp. pp. 44-54, which deal with the differences between Schleiermacher and Baur. Hodgson has also

translated selected writings of Baur's: *Ferdinand Christian Baur on the Writing of Church History*, A Library of Protestant Thought (New York: Oxford University Press, 1968).

[13]Heinrich Johann Theodor Schmid, "Über das Verhältnis der Theologie zur Philosophie," *FThPh* 1, 1 (1828): 16-73. Schmid claims (p. 58) that Schleiermacher gives to philosophy the same role that the Alexandrian and Scholastic theologians had given it. Philosophy is used merely as an external tool or auxiliary means to develop and to expound scientifically the church's faith, which is itself completely independent of philosophy.

Schleiermacher's observation that this charge is the opposite of that of gnosticism in fact approximates Schmid's own view of the matter. In "In wie fern darf der Schleiermachersche Standpunkt der Theologie mit dem gnostischen verglichen werden," *FThPh* 2, 1 (1829): 151-54, Schmid reviewed both Baur's inaugural dissertation and Karl Immanuel Nitzsch's review article, "Rec. Baur's *Primae rationalismi* (1827)," *ThStK* 1 (1828): 836-53. Although Schmid agrees with Baur about the parallel between gnosticism and Schleiermacher's theology, he suggests a twofold modification. First, the point of comparison lies in Schleiermacher's idealization of historical Christianity. Second, the label "gnostic" is more properly applied to Daub and Marheinecke than to Schleiermacher, for their method constructs the historical from the ideal, whereas Schleiermacher's constructs the ideal from the historical; i.e., he gives the historical a higher interpretation and meaning which is then identified as "ideal." This method is similar to Origen's method of interpreting the Bible allegorically. Philosophy is only the handmaid of theology because it takes faith as given and then explains or idealizes it into knowledge.

In "Ein Wort über Schleiermachers erstes Sendschreiben über seine Glaubenslehre an Dr. Lücke (in den *theol. Studien und Kritiken*, Band 2, Nr. 2)," *FThPh* 2, 3 (1829): 135-38, Schmid defended his interpretation of Schleiermacher in response to this letter to Lücke. He later published a full account of his view of Schleiermacher's thought: *Über Schleiermachers Glaubenslehre mit Beziehung auf die Reden über die Religion* (Leipzig: F. A. Brockhaus, 1835).

Biographical Note: Schmid (1799-1836) studied philosophy, history, and theology at the University of Jena. In 1830 he was named Professor of Philosophy and Philosophy of Religion at Heidelberg. A personal friend and philosophical follower of Jakob Friedrich Fries (see n. II, 53 below), Schmid was a major contributor and for a time editor of *FThPh*, the official organ of the Fries school.

[14]Baur, Bretschneider, and Tzschirner compare Schleiermacher with Schelling. For Tzschirner, see n. I, 7 above. Baur compares the two in the context of his discussion of Scheiermacher and gnosticism (*Comparatur*, p. 21; "Anzeige," pp. 257-58). There it is claimed that, just as Schelling distinguishes three principles in his conception of God, so Schleiermacher identifies three moments in the idea of God (see n. I, 28 below). Baur also argues that Schelling and Schleiermacher conceive of God by reference to successive stages in the development of human consciousness and affirm that the pre-Christian world is an under-developed stage and Christianity is the developed one. Both regard Christ as the one with a perfect consciousness of God. This view is said to be evident in the way Schleiermacher distributes the divine attributes throughout the whole system, so that the individual developmental moments of religious self-consciousness are correlated exactly with their objective expressions.

In *Die christliche Gnosis*, Baur contrasts Schleiermacher
and Schelling. Whereas Schelling admits a duality of principles,
i.e., a real distinction, within the divine being itself, and the
mediation of that duality through a series of moments or temporal
developments, Schleiermacher refuses to posit such distinctions
within the divine. What is objective for Schelling is subjective
in Schleiermacher. Since Schleiermacher holds that the divine is
present in the immediacy of feeling, he does not follow Schelling
in attributing concrete determinations to the divine nature itself.
       Not until the *Grundansichten* of 1828 does Bretschneider
associate Schleiermacher with Schelling, a fact which suggests
the possible influence of Baur's work (see n. I, 9 above).
Bretschneider considers Schelling's central philosophical point
to be that the evolution of the world is nothing else than God's
own evolution and coming to self-consciousness. This view he
attributes not only to Schelling, but also to Schleiermacher,
Marheinecke, and Hase. His analysis of their theologies is preceded by that of Schelling's philosophy. See *Grundansichten*,
pp. 12-14.

       [15]Rust, *De nonnullis*, p. 46. Schleiermacher's letter of March
30, 1818 to Jacobi sheds light on the relationship between the two.
For the text and a commentary, see Martin Cordes, "Der Brief
Schleiermachers an Jacobi: Ein Beitrag zu seiner Entstehung
und Überlieferung," *ZThK* 68 (1971): 195-212. A recent study of
the topic is available in Eilert Herms, *Herkunft, Entfaltung und
erste Gestalt des Systems der Wissenschaften bei Schleiermacher*
(Gerd Mohn: Gütersloher Verlagshaus, 1974), esp. pp. 119-63.
       Biographical Note: Jacobi (1743-1819) was known as a leading
advocate of a philosophy of feeling or faith and as a polemical
critic of the various rationally oriented philosophies of his
day--The Enlightenment, Kant, and post-Kantian idealism. With
Christoff Martin Wieland, he founded in 1764 the literary magazine
Der Merkur and there published his two literary works, *Allwills
Briefsammlung* (1774) and *Woldemar* (1779). The publication of his
conversations with Lessing, *Über die Lehre Spinozas in Briefen an
den Herrn Moses Mendelssohn* (Breslau: G. Löwe, 1785), produced a
revival of interest, both critical and appreciative, in Spinoza's
thought.
       In his literary works as well as in his deliberately unsys-
tematic philosophical statements, Jacobi sought to direct attention away from rational demonstration to the inner life and its
experience. He contended that the best uses of theoretical reason, as exhibited in Spinoza and Fichte, result in intellectually
consistent systems of atheistic pantheism. Such systems--as well
as that of Kant, which lacks even the virtue of consistency--fail
to recognize that human reason (*Vernunft*) apprehends supersensible
realities (the Good, the True, the Beautiful, and the personal God),
not mediately through demonstration, but immediately through
feeling or faith.

       [16]Bretschneider interprets Schleiermacher's understanding of
sin and the need for redemption as the foundation of an "unnatural
monkish morality." In his opinion, Schleiermacher's account of
sin as a conflict or antagonism between the sensible and spiritual
levels of human self-consciousness cannot be part of a Christian
world view, in which the sensible world and the sensible self-
consciousness are regarded as created by God. It fits rather
into a Manichaean world view. The moral consequence of this view,
according to Bretschneider, is that the senses and reason are set
into an unnatural and sinful relation to each other. Reason is
not permitted to acknowledge the rightful claims of the senses.
And, inasmuch as Schleiermacher makes the spiritual element

absolute, he lays the basis for a monastic spirituality. See "Über den Begriff der Erlösung," pp. 6-14; *Grundansichten*, pp. 28-30; "Bretschneider's View," pp. 608-610.

[17]Rust, *De nonullis*, p. 61, note. "Cyrenian" refers to the minor Socratic school founded by Aristippus at Cyrene, Africa. Like Epicureanism, it taught that pleasure is the true goal of life. Rust's accusation occurs in the context of his argument that Schleiermacher relies on subjective, rather than objective, criteria for religious truth. Schleiermacher's position is similar to that of the Cyrenians inasmuch as religious truth-claims are explained on the basis of sensation (feelings of pleasure and pain).

[18]Delbrück, *Erörterungen*, p. 120.

[19]Rust, *De nonnullis*, pp. 48-50. Rust refers to a passage in the First Speech in Schleiermacher's *On Religion*, pp. 47-48:
Now piety was, as it were, the maternal womb in whose sacred obscurity my young life was nourished and prepared for a world still closed to it. Before my spirit had found its distinctive sphere in the search for knowledge and in the mature experience of life, it found its vital breath in piety. As I began to sift out the faith of my fathers to clear the rubbish of former ages from my thoughts and feelings piety supported me. As the childhood images of God and immortality vanished before my doubting eyes piety remained. It led me headlong, without design, into an active adult life. It showed me how, with all my merits and defects, I was to retain sanctity by enjoying an integrated existence of my own.

[20]Rust argues that Schleiermacher had in no way relinquished that first piety of childhood because he understands piety as feeling rather than as knowledge.

[21]Christoph Benjamin Klaiber, "Über Begriff und Wesen des Supranaturalismus, und die Versuche, ihm mit dem Rationalismus zu vereinigen," *StGW* 1, 1 (1827): 73-156. An extensive footnote (n. 17, pp. 102-16) deals with Schleiermacher. Here (pp. 112-13) Klaiber finds a parallel between Schleiermacher's doctrine of God and his Christology. Just as God is not conceived as transcending the world, but as the impersonal, absolute, and ideal life in the world, i.e., as the highest point of human consciousness, "so is also Christ, the Logos of God (still prescinding from his appearance in a particular person), the most perfect revelation and explication of the divine life or the presentation of the idea of God in human consciousness in general." Klaiber suggests that this view places the historical Christ into the background because the revelation of Christ in the self or the divine life within human consciousness is prior to the historical Jesus, at least in its roots and origin. In support of his interpretation he refers to *CG*, [1]§§20,1; 110,1; 114; 121,3; 169; and 174,2.
   Biographical Note: Klaiber (1795-1836) was born in Württemburg and was educated at the University of Tübingen. As a professor at Tübingen from 1823 until 1836 and as a pastor in Stettin afterward, he championed the supernaturalist party and its point of view.

[22]Karl Immanuel Nitzsch, "Rec. Delbrück's Erörterungen," *ThStK* 1 (1828): 640-68. On p. 656, Nitzsch argues that, in contrast to such rationalists as Lessing, Kant, and Reinhard, Schleiermacher acknowledges the primal significance of faith. Cognizant of the presence of Christian faith in history prior to knowledge and speculation, Schleiermacher seeks to appropriate the most histori- cally faithful conception of Christianity, and he is critical of those elements of doctrine, e.g., "the Trinity and the doctrine of the pre-worldly Christ and Logos," that are already in their origins dogmatic and speculative.

Biographical Note: Nitzsch (1787-1868) was among the fore- most representatives of mediating theology (see n. I, 1 above), and in that capacity he served as editor of *ThStK*. Educated at Wittenberg, he was greatly influenced by the thought of Lessing and Kant, but later came under the influence of Schleiermacher and the romantics. He began his career in 1810 as a Lecturer in New Testament and Theology at Wittenberg. His work is pastoral theo- logy, however, gained him special distinction, and in 1817 he was named Professor of the *Predigerseminar* in Wittenberg. Five years later he became Professor of Pastoral Theology and Systematics at Bonn, where he remained until 1847 when the University of Berlin chose him to become Marheinecke's successor. Like Schleiermacher, he sought to provide a theoretical basis for pastoral theology (*Praktische Theologie,* 2 vols. [Bonn: Adolf Marcus, 1843-51]).

As advocate of the Union between Lutheran and Reformed, he helped found the *Deutsche Zeitschrift für christliche Wissenschaft und christliches Leben* (1850), which was dedicated to that cause. His main theological work, *System der christlichen Lehre für academische Vorlesungen* (Bonn: Adolf Marcus, 1832), was translated into English as *System of Christian Doctrine*, trans. from the 5th and rev. German ed. by Robert Montgomery and John Henn (Edinburgh: T & T Clark, 1849). A recent monograph on Nitzsch is by Henning Theurich, *Theorie und Praxis der Predigt bei Carl Immanuel Nitzsch* (Göttingen: Vandenhoeck & Ruprecht, 1977).

[23]Baur, "Anzeige," pp. 240-56, esp. pp. 150-52; *Comparatur,* p. 7. Baur argues that, although Schleiermacher interprets Christianity as centered in the consciousness of redemption de- rived from the person of Jesus of Nazareth (*CG,* [1]§18; [2]§11), his method and exposition are based on the idea of Christ as redeemer rather than on the historical Jesus. In Baur's opinion the methodological starting point is for Schleiermacher not the bibli- cal record, but the feeling of absolute dependence. The question is whether the redeemer is to be understood in terms of this per- sonally conceived idea of redemption or from the redeemer as actually given in history. Baur also contends that Schleier- macher's exposition is likewise determined by the principle set forth in *CG,* [1]§34 (cf. [2]§30), which stipulates that descriptions of human states are the fundamental form of dogmatic propositions. Baur concludes that Schleiermacher "gives Christ a purely ideal significance and in each case gives the historical Christ only a subordinate significance to the ideal Christ, just as the first and second forms of dogmatic propositions are related to one another."

[24]Klaiber, "Über Begriff und Wesen," pp. 113-14. Klaiber argues that for Schleiermacher the ideas of redemption and the redeemer are already given in the general consciousness of sin and there- fore appear prior to the historical Christ. (He cites as evidence *CG,* [1]§§21,3; 93; and 114). Moreover, the inner Christ comes to reality and develops insofar as God-consciousness becomes increas- ingly dominant within human awareness. Klaiber then concludes with the sentence to which Schleiermacher refers: "That inner

Christ, however, as a perfect development and presentation of the ideal, the divine in the real finite or as the highest development of the God-consciousness in humans, must also have appeared in a historical person if there was to be a real, perfect community of life between him and historically developing humanity, or if the total Christian life, a Christian church, was to be formed."

[25]Schleiermacher had written (*CG*, [1]§114,2; cf. [2]§93,3):

> If, on the other hand, one wanted to say that Christ, as he is presented in faith, is indeed archetypal, but that this appearance of the Son of God has been at all times only a spiritual reality in human souls and that the Son of God could not have appeared historically in an external, individual person, then one would consequently have to attribute to the human soul even in its condition of sinfulness the ability to produce a pure archetype. In that case, the idea of Christ would be only an imperfect archetype, and Christianity would have to be conceived as waiting for a higher development. If, however, human nature from itself, as existent, could produce a pure archetype, then it could not have been in the condition of sinfulness, because of the natural connection between the understanding and the will. Without sin, however, redemption would be nothing.

In short, since human nature in the condition of sin could not produce a perfect archetype, and since this archetype has been produced, it follows that the redeemer must have appeared in history. This argument Baur rejects. According to Baur, Schleiermacher has not convincingly established "why human nature could not produce out of itself a pure archetype" ("Anzeige," p. 252), but comes to this conclusion because of his theological presupposition that propositions about Christ belong to the first form of dogmatic propositions, whereas those about the historical Jesus belong to the second form. Schleiermacher's response is that he does not have such a presupposition and that his text has been twisted to say that opposite of what it means.

[26]See, e.g., the anonymous essay, "Bemerkungen über die Lehre von Gnadenwahl, in Beziehung auf Schleiermachers Abhandlung," *StGW* 1, 1 (1827): 175; and Albert Knapp, "Ist die Verschiedenheit der dogmatischen Systeme keine Hinderniss des Zwecks der Kirche?," *StGW* 1, 2 (1828): 126, which reads: "Already the principle of the aesthetic system, that other religions too have their salvation, although imperfect, indicates that there is no talk here of a salvation through Christ in the biblical and ecclesial [*kirchlichen*] sense at all, but only of one that consists in the moral imitation of the founder."
    The passage cited in the *CG* is not found on p. 213 of the original text but in [1]§121,1 (cf. [2]§100,3), where Schleiermacher argues against the purely "empirical point of view."
    Biographical Note: Knapp (1798-1864) was an evangelical pastor in Württemberg. A poet and littérateur, he is often referred to as the "spiritual Klopstock" of the nineteenth century. Advocating a biblically oriented religion of the heart, he warned against the intellectualism of much orthodoxy and the sterility of Enlightenment religion. A well-known hymnologist, he published several collections of older hymns, the most famous of which was his *Evangelische Liederschatz* (1837).

[27]Baur, *Comparatur*, p. 13.

[28]Ibid., p. 26; "Die Anzeige," p. 257.   Baur identifies three
moments in Schleiermacher's conception of God by reference to an
alleged dependence upon Schelling's philosophy.   Schelling distinguishes three principles: 1) God as the highest primordial
ground, the indifference, 2) nature or the real, the ground in God,
and 3) God in immanent meaning, i.e., God as Spirit or as Ideal.
Baur suggests that Schleiermacher likewise distinguishes three
moments in the idea of God: 1) absolute God in the most strict
sense, 2) God as God, without any relation to Christ as the Redeemer, and 3) God in Christ or the perfect idea of God through
the consciousness of redemption in Christ.

[29]Baur, *Comparatur*, p. 26.

[30]Baur, *Comparatur*, p. 21.   In a letter to Karl Heinrich Sack
dated 9 April, 1825, two years before Baur's Academic Address,
Schleiermacher stated: "Whoever does not believe that I hold
fast to the historical Christ has not understood a single word of
my book or my method."   See Schleiermacher, *Briefe an einen Freund*,
ed. Dr. Seifert (Weimar: Verlag Deutsche Christen, 1939), p. 281.

[31]Johann Christian Friedrich Steudel, "Die Frage über die Aus-
führbarkeit einer Annäherung zwischen der rationalistischen und
supranaturalistischen Ansicht mit besonderer Rücksicht auf den
Standpunkt der Schleiermacher'schen Glaubenslehre," *TZTh* 1 (1828),
Stück 1, pp. 74-199 and Stück 2, pp. 74-120.   Steudel's criticism
occurs in the context of his analysis of Schleiermacher's concept
of revelation.   He argues that Schleiermacher reduces revelation
to what is new and original.   Yet if Christianity denies that
Islam is revealed because that religion can be explained in terms
of its antecedents in Christianity, Judaism, and local religious
traditions, the same objection could be made against Christianity,
since elements of Christian doctrine can be traced to sources in
Judaism and elsewhere.
      Likewise, if Schleiermacher focuses upon the totality of
life that flows from Christ into humanity, could one not also say
that Islam evidences a similarly miraculous enthusiam for
Mohammed?   Could one not argue that the Islamic understanding of
piety according to which the sensible self-consciousness and the
spiritual self-conscousness are related is a covenant of reconciliation established by the Islamic faith?   Steudel concludes that
Schleiermacher's concept of revelation does not make it possible
to answer such questions (see Stück 1, pp. 192-94).
      Biographical Note: Steudel (1799-1837) studied philosophy,
theology, and oriental languages at Tübingen.   In 1805 he became
a tutor at the University, and during 1808-9 he studied Orientalis-
tics in Paris.   Promoted in 1805 to the post of Professor of
Theology, he taught biblical subjects in the theological faculty
and Near Eastern languages in the philosophical faculty.   After
1826 he also lectured on dogmatic theology and ethics.   He was a
firm advocate of biblical supernaturalism. In 1828 he founded the
Tübinger Zeitschrift für Theologie as the official organ of the
school.   See also n. II, 34 below.

[32]Cf. *CG*, [1]§16,3 and [2]§9,2.   The second edition adds two negative comments about Islam: first, that its "fatalistic character
reveals in the clearest manner a subordination of the moral to the
natural" and, second, that, although Mohammedism is as monotheis-
tic as Judaism and Christianity, it "unmistakeably expresses the
aesthetic type" of faith in contrast to the teleological type of
the other two religions.

[33]Bretschneider regards feeling and the immediate self-consciousness as allied but not identical. He argues that unconscious
feelings are present in plants or in humans who are in a state of
sleep or in a faint. Consciousness, however, is a knowledge of a
determination of our being, whether that determination relates to
a feeling, a thought, or an action. The feeling of a person in a
faint may be aroused by stimulants, but only when one becomes
aware of one's "I" is there self-consciousness. See "Über das
Princip," p. 7; *Grundansichten,* p. 15; and "Bretschneider's View,"
p. 559.

[34]Bretschneider holds that the essence of piety is not feeling,
but a combination of knowledge, action, and feeling.   Sense objects
are to be distinguished from ideas or religious objects. The former make impressions that produce either pleasure or pain.   Prior
to this impression upon us, no knowledge of the object is required.
An idea, however, must first be apprehended before it can influence
the feeling.   Otherwise one would have a feeling only of something
obscure or indefinite rather than a feeling of God. Therefore,
a knowledge of God rather than a feeling is essential to piety
("Über das Princip," pp. 9-16; *Grundansichten,* pp. 15-18;
"Bretschneider's View," pp. 599-601).

[35]John Cassian, *Conferences,* 10, 1-3; E. T.: Owen Chadwick, ed.,
Western Asceticism, Library of Christian Classics, vol. 12 (London:
SCM Press, 1958), pp. 234-36. Abbot Isaac's second conference on
prayer tells about the pastoral letter of Theophilus, Patriarch of
Alexandria in 399.   This letter not only announced the day of the
month on which Easter would be kept, but also criticized the heresy
of the Anthropomorphists who taught that God has the form of a
human, since Genesis 1:26 stated quite clearly, "Let us make man
after our image and likeness."   This letter ran into strong opposition among the monks of Scete.   Photinus, a learned deacon, was
brought in to instruct the monks about the true faith and his sermon underscores the unmeasurability, incomprehensibility, invisi-
bility, and incorporeality of God.   This sermon made a strong impression upon an old monk, Sarapion.   He was converted to the truth,
but as Cassian relates (p. 235):

> When we stood up to give thanks to the Lord in
> prayer, the old man felt mentally bewildered
> at having to pray, because he could no longer
> sense in his heart the anthropomorphic image
> of God which he had always before his mind's
> eye when praying.   Suddenly he broke into
> bitter weeping and sobbing, and throwing
> himself prostrate on the ground into groans,
> he cried: "Woe is me! They have taken my
> God away from me and I have none to grasp,
> and I know not whom to adore or to address."

[36]In his definition of religion (*Handbuch der Dogmatik,* 1:
1-3), Bretschneider distinguishes between a concept (*Begriff*)
of religion that abstracts from experience and an idea (*Idee*)
of religion that is constructed by reason independently of experience.   The concept of religion includes both the belief in
God and the veneration of God.   The idea of God is the "acknowledgement of a perfect, absolute being, upon which all being is
dependent, or the belief in the objective reality of the idea,
besides an appropriate manner of action for this faith" (p. 2).
Thus the primal element is neither feeling, as de Wette and Schleiermacher affirm, nor practical reason, as in Kant and his school,
but the acceptance of the idea of God and a belief in its reality.

[37]Tzschirner, *Briefe eines Deutschen*, pp. 32 and 37, where the word *Gesinnung*, here translated as "disposition," is used. The term is important in Kant's ethics:

> To have a good or an evil disposition as an inborn natural constitution does not here mean that it has not been acquired by the man who harbors it, that he is not the author of it, but rather, that is has not been acquired in time (that he has *always* been good, or evil, *from his youth up*.) The disposition, i.e., the ultimate subjective ground of the adoption of maxims, can be one only and applies universally to the whole use of freedom [*Religion within the Limits of Reason Alone*, p. 20].

In his introductory essay, "The Ethical Significance of Kant's Religion," p. cxvii, John R. Silber explains that

> the disposition is thus the enduring aspect of *Willkür*; it is *Willkür* considered in terms of the continuity and fullness of its free expression. It is the enduring pattern of intention that can be inferred from the many discrete acts of *Willkür* and reveals their ultimate motive.

[38]Tzschirner, *Briefe eines Deutschen*, p. 36.

[39]Tzschirner developed a chest ailment in 1823; he died on February 17, 1828.

[40]Cf. Schleiermacher, *Brief Outline*. In §§1-31, the relationship between theology and church government and that between a religious interest and a scientific spirit are emphasized. The point is that, since theology has a practical purpose and character, an ecclesial interest is a necessary presupposition of the theological profession.

[41]In Semler's own vocabulary there is a distinction and even competition between "public religion" and "private religion," as well as a corresponding distinction between "public official theology" and "private theology." Private theology means, to Semler, not a particular selection of church doctrines but rather a personal appropriation of Christian truth through thoughtful insight. Public or church theology is academic theology, belonging to teachers and professors. Although this church theology is put forward as obligatory and as a source of unity, Semler does not believe it should be because its demands are extraneous to the true rational appropriation of Christian knowledge by the individual. See his *Versuch einer freiern theologischen Lehrart* (Halle: Schwetschke und Sohn, 1771). For a recent discussion of Semler's notion of theology and Schleiermacher's relation to it, see Trutz Rendtorff, *Church and Theology*, trans. Reginald Fuller (Phil.: Westminster Press, 1966).
    Biographical Note: Johann Salomo Semler (1725-1792) was educated at Halle, where he became in 1725 Professor of Theology. The pietism of his youth gave way to a mild rationalism which he called *"theologia liberalis."* He is perhaps best known as an early and forceful advocate of intellectual freedom in the study of religion, as demonstrated by his historical critical study of the development of a canon, *Abhandlung von freier Untersuchung des Kanons*, 4 vols. (Halle: Schwetschke und Sohn, 1771-75).

[42]Christoph Friedrich von Ammon, *Summa theologiae christianae*
(Göttingen: H. Dieterich, 1802; [3]1816), p. 6. A German edition
appeared as *Inbegriff der evangelischen Glaubenslehre* (Göttingen:
H. Dieterich, 1805).

    Biographical Note: A rationalist theologian whose position
was influenced by Kant, Ammon (1776-1850) taught at Erlangen
(1792-94), Göttingen (1794-1804), and again at Erlangen (1804-13),
before becoming the successor of Franz Volkmar Reinhard as Preacher
in the High Court of Dresden in 1813. Most of his writings dealt
with biblical topics, but his dogmatics ranked next to Bretschneider's as the standard text of its day. It sought to analyze
the biblical tradition in the context of the history of religions
and to separate the timeless truths of the Bible from the forms of
expression common to persons in the biblical period. In his
Dresden office he took a more conservative theological and political stance, and the publication of some of these views on the
occasion of the Reformation Anniversary of 1817 led to a strident
literary debate with Schleiermacher. A brief account is given in
Martin Redeker, *Schleiermacher: Life and Thought*, trans. John
Wallhauser (Phil.: Fortress Press, 1973), pp. 190-91).

[43]Tzschirner, *Briefe eines Deutschen*, pp. 38ff.

[44]Schmid, "Über das Verhältnis," pp. 55-57. Schmid accuses
Schleiermacher and Twesten of confusing the practical purpose of
theological skill with the purely theoretical prupose of dogmatics.
Underlying this criticism is a specific conception of theology as
a scientific discipline. Schmid views the purpose of a theological science to be the uncovering of the truth that is contained
in the images and symbols of dogma. It therefore has a twofold
goal: it criticizes the positive form of dogma and it translates
religious truth into a scientific form. According to Schmid,
Schleiermacher bases dogmatics on the historical forms and images
of the eternal. Such an approach displays the ideal and practical
significance of doctrine, but it neither criticizes the historical
form nor uncovers the scientific truth within it. See also his
later book-length analysis of Schleiermacher, where this criticism
is developed: *Über Schleiermachers Glaubenslehre*, pp. 197-202.

[45]At the basis of the differences between Schmid and Schleiermacher is a different conception of the status of natural religion. Schmid argues that Schleiermacher underestimates the significance of natural religion in relation to positive religion because he attributes to it only a subordinate or derivative role.
According to Schmid, Schleiermacher is correct to see that the relationship between positive and natural religion parallels that
between positive law and natural law. For Schleiermacher every
civil society is based on positive rather than natural law. Likewise, a religious society is based on positive rather than natural
religion. Yet Schmid believes that Schleiermacher is wrong in
saying that natural law and natural religion are only an abstrac-
tion from positive law and positive religion. In Schmid's view,
natural religion represents the universality and the validity of
positive religion; i.e., it contains those elements that lay
universal and necessary claim on all humans. In these terms
Schmid's dogmatics seeks to interpret the truth of religion in its
scientific form. See "Über das Verhältnis," pp. 65-73; "Ein
Wort über Schleiermachers erstes Sendschreiben," pp. 135-38; and
Über Schleiermachers Glaubenslehre, pp. 122-27.

[46]In discussing the relation between philosophy and theology,
Schmid focuses on the issue of the relationship between what is
rational and what is historical or positive. He divides contemporary opinions into three classes. The first develops the

positive into the rational, a position attributed to Schleiermacher and Twesten (cf. n. I, 44 above). The second, the "natural
philosophical," associates or constructs a positive, historical
faith out of philosophy. He associates this position with the
Hegelians, especially Marheinecke. The third amounts to a symbolic interpretation of a positive, historical faith according to
philosophical conceptions. In this letter to Lücke, Schleiermacher identifies Schmid's position with the second option. Schmid,
however, denies the identification because he claims to accept the
positive while subjecting it to scientific criticism and seeking
to discover its essential meaning ("Über das Verhältnis," pp.
53-73).

In "Ein Wort über Schleiermachers erstes Sendschreiben,"
pp. 137-38, Schmid explicitly rejects the charge that he constructs
the positive out of philosophy, pointing out that he attributed
that same opinion to others and criticized it. Insofar as the
positive is historically given and empirically perceivable, it
is independent of the rational. Nonetheless it must be subject
to philosophical criticism. His own dogmatics does not involve
a "sublimation into airy regions," but accepts the primal religious
feeling, the riches of history, and positive Christianity. It
does, however, subject all three to scientific criticism. See
also *Über Schleiermachers Glaubenslehre*, pp. 165-202, where Schmid
compares in detail the differences between his understanding of
dogmatics and that of Schleiermacher.

[47]In Plato the indemonstrable logos refers to the sphere of
cognition reached by the method of dialectic, whereby an account
(logos) of a Form is attained by the movement of the argument
itself rather than by means of sense images or illustrations (*The
Republic*, 6. 509-11). Here Plato correlates four regions of the
intelligible world and the world of appearances with four states
of mind or modes of cognition: 1) images of things are related
to imaging (*eikasia*), which takes appearances at face value;
2) visible things are correlated with belief (*pistis*); 3) mathe-
matical objects, with discursive reasoning (*dianoia*) that employs
diagrams as illustrations; and 4) the Forms, with dialectic,
which brings knowledge (*episteme*) or intelligence (*noesis*).
In dialectic the mind ascends without the aid of any illustrations
from certain premises to the first principle upon which the premises depend and, if the effort is successful, could then descend
by deduction to confirm the entire body of knowledge. See the
helpful account in Francis Macdonald Cornford's translation,
The Republic of Plato (New York and London: Oxford University
Press, 1941), pp. 221-23.

[48]Cf. *CG*, 1§9 and 2§4. The changes, especially the additions,
indicate how Schleiermacher attempts in the second edition to
emphasize how human freedom coexists with absolute dependence.

[49]Several reviewers contended that Schleiermacher's theology
destroys human dignity because it eliminates human freedom. For
example, Rust, *De nonnullis*, pp. 69-71, raises this point, as he
describes what is, according to him, Schleiermacher's pantheistic
account of the relation between God and the world.

Likewise, Johann Gottlieb Rätze, *Erläuterungen einiger
Hauptpunkte in Dr. Friedrich Schleiermachers christlichen Glaubenslehre nach den Grundsätzen der evangelischen Kirche im Zusammenhange dargestellt* (Leipzig: Wilhelm Lauffer, 1823), chap. 10,
claims that, if Schleiermacher's view of God as the author of sin
is accepted, then human freedom is negated. He concludes that
absolute dependence cannot be reconciled with human freedom and
that Schleiermacher reduces human agency to a natural mechanism.

If, however, sin is considered an act of human freedom, then its
cause should be attributed solely to the human being and not to
God.
    Biographical Note: Rätze (1790-1839) studied philosophy and
theology at the University of Leipzig. For a time he was a private
tutor until gaining a teaching post in a *Hochschule.* His publications were directed primarily to the dissemination and defense of
Kantianism. He was perhaps best known because of involvement in
the controversy sparked by Klaus Harms. A strict confessionalist,
Harms marked the Reformation Anniversary celebration of 1817 by
issuing *Ninety-Five Theses,* which condemned, among other things,
the reliance of modern theology upon reason rather than upon supernatural revelation. In response to this attack, Rätze undertook
to defend rational religion in *Der Thesestreit oder Harms und
seine Gegner: Ein Beitrag zur Beendigung des Streites zwischen der
Vernunftreligion und dem Offenbarungsglauben* (Leipzig: Lahnhold,
1818).

[50]Klaiber, "Über Begriff und Wesen," argues that a pantheistic
interpretation of divine omniscience and omnipotence cannot be
reconciled with human freedom. If human freedom is to be real,
and not merely formal, there must be an act of divine self-limitation in which the creator wills to create free, independent
beings. This limitation is not forced upon the divine will by
external principles, as in Manichaeanism, but springs from within
God's will itself (pp. 118-24).

[51]Steudel, "Die Frage," Stück 1, pp. 96-108. Steudel confronts
Schleiermacher's definition of piety directly. It is not sufficient,
he claims, to say that piety is a feeling of absolute dependence.
First, piety entails an acknowledgement of or consent to the
validity of this dependence. It is, then, primarily a directed-
ness of the self, by the self, toward its condition. Second, this
acknowledgement assumes that there is something higher and superior to the human self, so that piety implies a world view as well
as a specification of the human will. Third, piety as redefined
involves a different relationship between dependence and human
freedom than that which Schleiermacher describes.

[52]Friedrich Daniel Ernst Schleiermacher, *Die christiche Sitte
nach den Grundsätzen der evangelischen Kirche im Zusammenhange
dargestellt. Aus Schleiermachers handschriftlichen Nachlass und
nachgeschriebene Vorlesungen,* ed. Ludwig Jonas, *SW,* 1, 12. During
his career Schleiermacher lectured twelve times on the subject
matter of "*christliche Sittenlehre*" or "*christliche Moral.*"
As early as 1820 he considered published the lectures, as indicated in Schleiermacher an einen Halle'schen Schüler, 26 February
1810, *ASL,* 4:177. See also *ASL,* 4:184, 208, and 237. The best
recent study is Hans-Joachim Birkner, *Schleiermachers christliche
Sittenlehre im Zusammenhange seines philosophisch-theologischen
Systems* (Berlin: Alfred Töpelmann, 1964).

[53]Since Steudel contended that piety requires both a cogni-
tional element or world view and a volitional direction and
acknowledgement, he concluded that Schleiermacher is "in no way
justified to claim that religion or piety has its roots more
immediately in feeling than in willing and knowing" ("Die Frage,"
Stück 1, p. 100).

[54]Ibid.

[55]Ibid., pp. 101-2. Steudel took issue with Schleiermacher's
definition of piety as absolute dependence as well as with his
rejection of an interaction between the finite person and the

totality of the universe. Although Steudel concedes that humans
cannot conceive of themselves apart from this dependency, he
argues that they are nevertheless conscious of a freedom to realize
the divine order. This freedom is an ability to act upon and to
affect the universe, although always in accord with the divine
plan. Despite Schleiermacher's rhetorical question here, he does
introduce considerable modifications on this point in the 2d ed.
of the *CG*. See n. I, 56 below.

[56]Ibid., pp. 102-3. In criticizing Schleiermacher's definition
of piety, Steudel asks if self-consciousness and absolute dependence
can coexist. Self-consciousness requires a consciousness of one's
subsistence, and indeed of a subsistence that is not dependent
upon the existence of another. An absolute dependence would seem
to rule out the consciousness of self, as self-subsisting. In
fact, Schleiermacher revised his definition of piety in order to
defend himself against the charge that he excluded human freedom
and self-consciousness (cf. *CG*, [1]§9,3 and [2]§4,2).

[57]Bretschneider argued that knowledge or apprehension rather
than feeling is the primal element of piety. If the correlate
to absolute dependence were to be absolute infinity, this infinity
would be only an indeterminate notion of irresistible power.
Unless that power were apprehended as good and wise, it would ex-
cite only fear and trembling rather than love or trust. In Bretschneider's opinion, then, it is through this apprehension that
reason brings the idea of God to consciousness, and only on this
basis can there be a foundation for Christian piety with its faith
in the love of God. "Thus it appears," concludes Bretschneider,
"that Schleiermacher's conception of religion can never be the
foundation of a theory of the Christian faith." See *Grundansichten*, pp. 17-18; "Bretschneider's View," pp. 600-1; and "Über das
Prinzip," pp. 21-22.

[58]Schleiermacher notes that he defines absolute dependence not
in [1]§10 of the *CG* ([2]§5) but in [1]§9 ([2]§4). [1]§9 reads" "The common
element of all pious affections, that which is the essence of
piety, is that we are conscious of ourselves as absolutely dependent. . . ." [1]§10 states: "Piety is the highest stage of human
feeling, which takes up the lower, but is not present apart from
it." In the second edition, both propositions are revised.

[59]Bretschneider argues that without some prior conception of
God as the object of the feeling of absolute dependence, the
feeling would be obscure and indefinite. Hence all obscure feelings, and not only that of absolute dependence, could be considered
piety. (Cf. n. I, 57 above.) See "Über das Prinzip," pp. 16-17;
"Bretschneider's View," p. 600.

[60]Bretschneider, "Über das Princip," pp. 19-20; *Grundansichten*,
p. 18; "Bretschneider's View," p. 601.

[61]In support of his claim that knowledge of God rather than
feeling is essential to piety, Bretschneider cites the further
reason that only through reflection can humans become conscious
of absolute dependence. In line with his arguments that feelings
need not be conscious, Bretschneider claims that in feelings the
self experiences present limitations and restraints. One experiences an inability to overcome a restraint at a given moment:
the feeling does not mean that the restraint cannot be overcome
at all. In order to distinguish between a relative restraint
that can be overcome and an absolute restraint that cannot

be overcome, it is necessary for reason to comprehend the limitation *as* absolute. See "Über das Princip," pp. 17-18: *Grundansichten*, p. 17; and "Bretschneider's View," p. 600.

[62]According to Bretschneider (*Grundansichten*, p. 21: "Bretschneider's View," p. 603), Schleiermacher bases the necessity of
redemption on the contradiction or antagonism in the human self
between the pious feeling and the sensuous feeling. This conflict,
Bretschneider argues, is attributed by Schleiermacher to the human
desire "to constitute a personal or individual sensuous life," and
it ". . . can be removed only by both feelings becoming in the
same moment one; and this union can be affected only when the
higher (the pious) feeling 'takes up' the lower (the sensuous)
feeling into itself (*in sich aufnehme*)"
    Cf. *CG*, [1]§10 and [2]§5. Even in the first edition, Schleier-
macher stresses that his language about the distinct levels of
self-consciousness is to be understood "figuratively" (*uneigentlich*)
and that the higher self-consciousness always exists as temporally
determined, i.e., connected to the sensible self-consciousness.
The second edition emphasizes the coexistence (*zugleichgesetz-
sein*) of the two and explains that they do not melt (*verschmelzen*)
into one another, but are co-present. One is never conscious of
absolute dependence as such, but always as it is specifically
modified by the sensible self-consciousness ([2]§5,3).

[63]Bretschneider maintains that Schleiermacher's treatment of
original sin abandons the path of "psychological speculation on
which his system is based" and turns to "the province of outward
experience" alone. Since Schleiermacher teaches that sin is not
essential to human nature and, therefore, that it is possible for
humans either to sin or not to sin, he must explain why in fact
all individuals realize only the possibility of sinning. His explanation, however, is not based on an analysis of immediate self-
consciousness, as his methodology would dictate, but on historical
and empirical observations about the characteristics of different
groups of persons, nations, and races. In Bretschneider's opinion,
such appeals are totally inconsistent with the methodological
starting point of the Introduction to the *CG*. See *Grundansichten*,
pp. 32-34; "Bretschneider's View," pp. 612-13.

[64]"Nor do I seek to understand, in order that I may believe,
but I believe, in order that I may understand. For he who does not
believe, does not experience, and he who does not experience,
does not understand." (Anselm, *Proslogion*, 1; *de fide Trin.*, 2;
see *CG*, title page.

[65]Schleiermacher, *Brief Outline*, §§195-96 and 219, emphasizes
that personal conviction and experience are necessary for undertaking the task of dogmatic theology.

[66]Bretschneider, *Grundansichten*, p. 20 ("Bretschneider's View,"
p. 602):

> The feeling of absolute dependence, or the pious
> feeling, the author calls the God's-consciousness,
> or the Divine consciousness (*Gottesbewusstsein*),
> which is not to be confounded with the conscious-
> ness, that is, the knowledge of God. When he main-
> tains that this pious feeling, or Divine conscious-
> ness, is innate in man, and always existing in him,
> he means that it is the immanent life of God him-
> self, manifested in man in the form of spiritual
> consciousness.

[67]*CG*, 1§117,2: ". . . . the distinction between the Redeemer
and all other persons has been defined such that, instead of our
impure and clouded God-consciousness, there was in Him a pure
being of God under the form of consciousness and conscious
activity. . . ." Cf. 2§96,3: "For if the distinction between
the Redeemer and the rest of us is established in such a way that,
instead of being obscured and powerless as in us, the God-consciousness in Him was absolutely clear and determined each moment,
to the exclusion of all else, so that it must be regarded as a
continual living presence, and withal a real existence of God
in Him, then, in virtue of this difference, there is in Him everything we need. . . ."

[68]Baur, "Anzeige," pp. 250-53; *Comparatur*, pp. 15 and 23.

[69]Nitzsch, "Rec. Baur's *Primae rationalismi* (1827), " *ThStK* 1
(1828): 836-53. On pp. 848-52, Nitzsch defends Schleiermacher's
method and his Christology against Baur's charge that Schleiermacher fails to take seriously the historical Jesus. Baur had
pointed to the omission of a historical analysis of the Gospel
texts in the *CG*. Nitzsch responds that such an analysis belongs
more properly to apologetical than to dogmatic theology and therefore had no place in the *CG*. He argues, moreover, that it is not
possible by means of historical-biblical studies to prove that
Jesus is the Christ. Such an attempt would reduce the proof of the
truth of Christianity to an empirical demonstration. The belief
in Jesus as the Christ is more than a collection of gospel materials
on Jesus. Nitzsch also points to the inadequacy of Baur's interpretation of Schleiermacher's Christology. To view it, as Baur
does, as a naturalistic account of the human projection of the need
for a redeemer is to overlook Schleiermacher's own criticisms of
naturalistic conceptions of the redeemer.

[70]Analyzing the treatment of revelation in the *CG*, 1§19 (cf.
2§10, appendix), Braniss argues that Schleiermacher cannot demonstrate the uniqueness of Christ vis-à-vis all other humans. Since
Schleiermacher's concept of revelation does not permit him to distinguish religion from any other aspect of human culture, every
creative human work, as something new and irreducible to its historical antecedents, may be regarded as "revealed." How, then,
does the status of Jesus differ from that of Aristotle? The
teachings of both can be seen as something new, or they can be
traced back to antecedents in Greek and Hebrew thought. Schleiermacher's attempt to avoid the consequences of this view by appealing to the broad influence and efficacy of Christ for changing
human life is not convincing, for, according to Braniss, a similar
influence has been exercises upon posterity by Aristotle. See
Über Schleiermachers Glaubenslehre, pp. 104-8.

[71]*CG*, 1§188,3 and 2§98,1.

[72]Bretschneider takes issue (*Grundansichten*, pp. 37-38; "Bretschneider's View," pp. 615-16) with Schleiermacher's understanding
of sin as a conflict between the lower and the spiritual levels
of self-consciousness because, given this view, one would have to
attribute sin even to Jesus. Schleiermacher maintained that at no
time did Jesus experience such a conflict, but Bretschneider contends that this claim is "inconsistent with the Gospel history,"
where "there are recorded moments in the life of Jesus when he
felt, and actually was, in conflict, as a man, and consequently,
according to the theory of the author, sinned" ("Bretschneider's
View," p. 615). With Schleiermacher he is willing to overlook
the story of the temptations of Christ, although it is "probably

a parabolic representation of an inward temptation." But the
scene in Gethsemane, the cry on the cross, and other passages
(Mt. 26.37-38 and Heb. 5.7) indicate a struggle within Jesus.

[73]Braniss argues that certain dangerous consequences result
from Schleiermacher's conception of the relation between revelation and history. For example, divine revelation cannot be so
demarcated that one knows whether it is an immediate effect of
God or a product of the general course of history. Each revelation appearing within the nexus of history has two sides. It expresses a new power or impulse for development, and it expresses
an idea that is to be realized.

In Christianity, redemption appears as a new power of development in the human race to overcome its restraints, i.e., the
power to liberate the God-consciousness from the yoke of sensible
self-consciousness. Redemption as an idea is that of a spirit
totally free from the restraints of nature. Although the idea
may appear at any point in history, the power of redemption will
determine history only at the end of its total development. Thus
in Jesus Christ the idea of redemption can be given immediately
as a complete and perfect idea, but the power of redemption can
exist only in a relatively limited way characteristic of a beginning stage of development. In this sense the power of redemption
in Jesus must be called a minimum rather than a maximum. According to Braniss, this conclusion is the logical outcome of Schleiermacher's conception of the relation between divine causality and
human history. (See *Über Schleiermacher's Glaubenslehre*, pp.
192-94; cf. n. I, 5 above for the same issue in relation to the
sinlessness of Christ.)

[74]Brannis, *Über Schleiermacher's Glaubenslehre*, pp. 196-97.
Braniss believes that such a view follows necessarily from
Schleiermacher's conception of divine causality. Either Jesus is
totally removed from the nexus of nature and history or is fully
within it. In the former case, Schleiermacher cannot maintain
his view of divine causality; in the latter case he can.

[75]Nitzsch, "Rec. Delbrück's Erörterungen," p. 632. In response
to Delbrück's charge that Schleiermacher's teaching is irreconcilable with apostolic teaching, Nitzsch compares Schleiermacher's
exposition with the three articles of The Apostles' Creed. He
concludes that the creedal articles are more adequately maintained
in Schleiermacher's work than in that of the rationalistic neologi-
cal theology of the eighteenth century. This is especially true
with respect to Christology, for the neologians transformed belief
in Christ into a belief in providence, virtue, immortality, or the
so-called teachings of Jesus, whereas Schleiermacher makes
Christology the basic article, of his *Glaubenslehre*.

[76]These are Baur's criticisms of Schleiermacher; see "Anzeige,"
pp. 256-59, and *Comparatur*, p. 26.

[77]Nitzsch, "Rec. Delbrück's Erörterungen," p. 657. Responding
to Delbrück's accusation that Schleiermacher is a pantheist, Nitzsch
suggests that a certain pantheism (*ein gewisser Pantheism*) arises
from biblical-Christian monotheism, insofar as Christianity teaches
the unity of the supernatural and the natural and maintains that
in nature there is a repeated annulment of secondary causality.
According to Nitzsch, it is not surprising, then, to find that
biblical concepts have often converged with those of the later
Stoics, the Pythagoreans, the Platonists, and Spinoza. Nitzsch
cites as a confirmation of his opinion Augustine's remarks on the
close relationship between Christianity and Platonism.

[78]The term "pantheism" first served to designate English Deism,
and only toward the end of the eighteenth century, stimulated
especially by Jacobi, were deism and pantheism contrasted. See
H. Scholz, "Zur ältesten Begriffsgeschichten von Deismus und
Pantheismus," *Preussiche Jahrbücher* 142 (1910): 318-25. Recently,
H. Timm has shown that under Jacobi's influence the term "pantheism" came to be used polemically to refer to the "one and all
doctrine" of neo-Spinozists, Lessing, and Goethe. See H.
Timm, *Gott und die Freiheit, I: Studien zur Religionsphilosophie
der Goethezeit* (Frankfurt: Vittorio Klostermann, 1974), p. 139.

[79]Tzschirner, *Briefe eines Deutschen*, p. 26. Here Schleiermacher is associated with international romanticism which, it is
claimed, grounds religion in artistic expressivity and aesthetics.
See also n. II, 28 below.

[80]Christian Friedrich Böhme (1766-1844) was the author of an
anonymous review of the *CG* that appeared in the *Allgemeine
Literatur-Zeitung* 115-17 (May 1823): 49-72. Schleiermacher referred to this review in two letters, one to Lücke dated June 18,
1823 and the other to Gass dated December 20, 1823 (*ASL*, 4:313-15
and 318-21, respectively). In the former letter he complains
that this review with its accusations of pantheism was perhaps
excerpted and included in a report sent by the ministry of police
to the ministry of education. In the letter to Gass he labels
this review "sophistic gossip."
    Biographical Note: Böhme was a pastor, first in Altenberg
(1800-13) and then in Lucka. His publications dealt mainly with
biblical topics, e.g., commentaries on *Romans* and on *Hebrews* and
a study of the religion of Jesus, and with analyses of contemporary theology.

[81]In the Introduction to the *CG*, [1]§2,2 and [2]§16, Postscript,
Schleiermacher underscores the point that Christian theology must
seek increasingly to keep itself free from any philosophy, worldly
wisdom, and natural theology. The greatest disadvantage in any
alliance among them is that theological propositions could come
to be considered philosophical propositions and vice versa. For
a recent treatment of this complex issue with ample documentation
from Schleiermacher's writings and recent literature, see Hans-
Joachim Birkner, *Theologie und Philosophie*, Theologische Existenz
Heute, No. 178 (Munich: Chr. Kaiser Verlag, 1974).

[82]Baur, Bretschneider, and Tzschirner associated Schleiermacher with Schelling (see n. I, 14 above). The reference is
here most probably to Bretschneider, *Grundansichten*, pp. 12-14,
where it is argued that both Schelling and Schleiermacher see in
Christianity the history of the temporally developing personality
of God; i.e., they regard the history of the world and of the
human spirit as the revelation of the evolving divine nature. The
incarnation represents for both the union of the divine and human
consciousness. Sin and original sin are understood as the separation of the individual from the absolute; reconciliation is the
return of the opposites to unity. The life of holiness consists
in the surrender of individual consciousness to the divine all.
Eschatology refers to the dissolution of all opposition into the
evolving divine personality.

[83]Klaiber, "Über Begriff und Wesen," pp. 100-2, argues that
that distinction between mediate and immediate, natural and supernatural, revelation rests upon a correct view of the relationship
between God and the world. He claims that Schleiermacher rejects
every mediate working of God in the world and regards all
phenomena as immediate effects of God. He also concludes that

Schleiermacher's view "can be consequently founded only upon the
denial of the true distinction between the finite and infinite
and upon the affirmation that the world is only the explication of
the divine life itself, only the divided and finitely formed
infinity." Therefore the causality of nature and that of God are
only formally distinguished, and the divine "is the true being of
all things and constitutes the inherent or immanent ground of their
being and life" (p. 102).

The second proposition appears on p. 103, n. 17: "Since
now this infinite life, like all life, consists of the mutual
interaction of diverse (attractive and expansive) forces, since
it therefore attains a revelation, a development, a becoming,
so the ground of the world is therefore based on this."

[84]Schleiermacher, *On Religion*, pp. 93-95.

[85]*CG*, [1]§15,5: In both editions of *CG*, Schleiermacher claims
that no historic church community has been based on pantheism and
that the term itself arose an a taunt or nickname rather than as
an expression of an actual religious group. In addition, *CG*,
[1]§15,5, states: ". . . pantheism must also be uniformly conceived
and held to the usual formula one and all (*hen kai pan*), and it
must then be admitted that the piety of a pantheist can be completely the same as that of a monotheist and that the difference
between pantheism and the generally current notion [of monotheism]
lies at the level of speculation."

The revision in *CG*, [2]§8, Postscript 2, states the same point
but with new accents:

> It is admitted that it [pantheism] does not . . .
> spring from the religious emotions, by direct
> reflection upon them. But it may be asked whether,
> having once arisen in some other way--by the way
> of speculation or simply of reasoning--it is yet
> compatible with piety. To this question an
> affirmative answer may be given without hesitation,
> provided that Pantheism is taken as expressing
> some variety or form of Theism, and that the word
> is not simply and solely a disguise for a mater-
> ialistic negation of Theism. . . . Let us accord-
> ingly hold Pantheism fast to the usual formula of
> One and All: then God and world will remain distinct
> at least as regards function, and thus such a man,
> since he reckons himself as belonging to the world,
> can feel himself, along with this All, to be dependent
> ln that which is the corresponding One. Such states
> of mind can scarcely be distinguished from the
> religious emotions of many of monotheist.

The passage referring to Spinoza in *On Religion* (p. 84)
reads:

> Join me, won't you, in offering a reverent tribute to
> the spirit of that saintly outcase Spinoza! The
> supreme Spirit of the world permeated his being;
> the infinite was his beginning and end; the universe
> was his sole and everlasting love. In sacred
> innocence and deep humility he saw himself mirrored
> in the world of the eternal and perceived how he him-
> self was its most worthy image. He was full of
> religion, of the Holy Spirit. And at that spot,
> therefore, he stands alone, unequaled: master of
> his craft, yet transcendent over profane society,
> possessing neither disciples nor citizenship.

[86]Delbrück, *Erörterungen,* p. 77.

[87]Debrück's "insinuations" are made in his *Erörterungen,* p. 110, n. 4. For Schleiermacher's challenge, see Schleiermacher to Gass, 22 November 1826, in *ASL* 4: 357-61. Except for the opening and closing paragraphs, this letter was printed in Sack, Nitzsch, and Lücke, *Über das Ansehen,* as an Appendix entitled, "Erklärung des Herrn der Schleiermacher über die ihn betreffenden Stellen der Streitschrift."
        In this Appendix (pp. 213-26), Schleiermacher defends himself against Delbrück's charge of pantheism or Spinozism. He notes that Delbrück had overlooked the third edition of *On Religion,* which contained a footnote (pp. 159-60) that sheds light on his judgment of Spinoza. In that note, p. 160, Schleiermacher asserts that the attention brought to Spinoza by Jacobi did not touch on what is most distinctive to Spinoza, and he explains that his own comments about Spinoza in the first edition of *On Religion* expressed--admittedly, in rather youthful terms--his respect for the piety of a man whom "the prosaic" of the day called "godless." "To me," he states, "the mind and heart of this great man seemed to be permeated with piety, even though it was not Christian piety."
        He then adds:

> How was I to anticipate what happened: that because
> I ascribed piety to Spinoza I would be taken for a
> Spinozist myself! This occured despite the fact
> that I had never in any way defended his system,
> despite the fact that anything philosophical in my
> book so obviously fails to jibe with what is dis-
> tinctive in his point of view.

        In the Appendix to *Über das Ansehen,* Schleiermacher argues that Delbrück should have shown where some of Spinoza's distinctive propositions, e.g., God as an extended being, the parallel between the relation of body and mind and that of object and notion, and the selfless love of God, are to be found in Schleiermacher's work. He is confident that none will be found.

[88]Delbrück, *Erörterungen,* p. 110, n.4. The use of images from the natural sciences to express forms of combination and connection was popular in the early nineteenth century. According to Jack Forstman, "in elective affinity two elements that have a strong 'attraction' for one another will join although each is compounded with another element." The term appears in early works of Friedrich Schlegel and gained special currency from Goethe's 1807 novel, *Elective Affinities.* See Forstman, *A Romantic Triangle: Schleiermacher and Early German Romanticism,* AAR Studies in Religion, ed. Stephen D. Crites, no. 13 (Missoula, MT: Scholars Press, 1977), p. 6.

[89]The penultimate section of the *CG* deals with the divine attributes of love and wisdom, which relate to grace and salvation ([1]§§180-85; [2]§§164-69); the section on the trinity concludes the system ([1]§§186-190; [2]§§170-72).

[90]Delbrück, *Erörterungen,* p. 100. In order to be in accord with Schleiermacher's position the familiar verse,

> What our God had created
> That he seeks also to preserve
> Over it both early and late
> He wills to hold sway with his grace,

should be rewritten as follows:

> *Even* what God had *not* created
> that he *must* indeed preserve
> over it both early and late
> he *must* with his *power* hold sway.

The changes (in our italics) indicate that for Delbrück, Schleiermacher denies creation as well as God's freedom in the preservation of the world and substitutes a necessity of power for the
freedom of grace.

In *Der verewigte Schleiermacher*, pp. 44-46, Delbrück admits
that Schleiermacher often refers to divine grace. But since in
Delbrück's view this divine grace is related to sin and not to
the preservation of the world, the verse is correct in this respect. He concedes that the term "must" was perhaps inappropriate,
so that the verse should read:

> Even what God had not created
> That he *does* preserve
> Over it both early and late
> He sways with his power.

Expressed in this way, God's activity could be interpreted either
as free, or as necessary, or as partially free and partially necessary, or as neither free nor necessary. Delbrück attributes this
latter view, which he calls a meaningless, i.e., an inconceivable,
idea, to Schleiermacher.

[91]*CG*, 1§68,3-5; 2§54,3-4. Schleiermacher contends that the
concept of divine omnipotence is endangered when one seeks to
distinguish between God's active and inactive will or between
God's free and necessary will. These distinctions should not be
applied to God, for one should be able to say that in God nothing
is necessary without at the same time being free and that nothing
is free without at the same time being necessary.

[92]Schleiermacher an Delbrück, 2 January 1827, in *ASL*, 4:371-77.
Here Delbrück's concept of God is said to be that of a chess
player who for every conceivable move has another move in mind, so
that checkmate will be infallibly achieved. Schleiermacher also
argues that Delbrück cannot solve the problem of the relation between human free will and divine omnipotence by appealing to the
"rule of faith" of the early church, but only by finding a "more
adequate approximation" in classical antiquity. Indeed, according to Schleiermacher, the rule of faith does not serve to resolve
the issue. But Delbrück's position is that of an eclectic between
Christianity and Hellenistic philosophy. See pp. 373-74.

[93]On p. 155 of his *Erörterungen*, Delbrück refers to Schleiermacher as a "Spinozistic wit" precisely because Schleiermacher
has used the image of God as a chess player to ridicule Delbrück's
conception of God. See also n. I, 92 above and Delbrück, *Der
verewigte Schleiermacher*, pp. 42-43.

[94]Delbrück, *Erörterungen*, pp. 87ff.

[95]Ibid., p. 87.

[96]Ibid., p. 7.

[97]The principle is Schleiermacher's teaching about the interrelation of freedom and necessity with regard to statements about
divine causality. See n. I, 91 above.

[98]Nitzsch, "Rec. Delbrück's *Erörterungen*," p. 656: "But he
[Schleiermacher] seeks as much as others always and only to incorporate what is distinctively Christian into a universal religious
knowledge, and he strives just as much for their highest unity
and agreement."

[99]By the middle of the eighteenth century, the reconciliation
between reason and revelation developed by Gottfried Wilhelm
Leibnitz (1646-1716) and Christian Wolff (1679-1754) had become a
dominant option in many German universities and among the educated
classes generally. A well-known mathematician, philosopher, and
statesman, Leibnitz defended Christianity against skepticism and
maintained a reputation for orthodoxy despite the predominantly
rationalistic cast of his system. In his opinion, the universe
was a harmoniously regulated system of elements that evidenced a
divine designer. In a book of 1709, *Theodicy: Essays on the Good-
ness of God, the Freedom of Man, and the Origin of Evil*, ed.
Austin Farrer, trans. E. M. Huggard (New Haven: Yale University
Press, 1953), he argued that God, who is perfect, must ordain
this best of all possible worlds. Evil, therefore, is but a means
to a higher good.
     Although an independent thinker in his own right, Wolff was
known primarily as a popularizer of the Leibnitzian point of view.
The pietists caused his dismissal from Halle in 1723, but his re-
appointment there by Frederick the Great in 1743 was seen as a
triumph of enlightenment. A popular teacher and author of such
works as *Logita oder Vernunft: Gedanken von der kräften des menschlichen Verstandes* (Halle: Renger, 1712) and *Vernünftige Gedanken
von Gott, der Welt und der Seele des Menschen, auch all Dingen
Überhaupt* (Frankfurt: Andrea, 1720), Wolff's influence was extensive both during and after his lifetime. By lecturing and writing
in German rather than Latin, he shaped decisively the philosophical
vocabulary of the day. The term Leibnitz-Wolffian theology, first
coined by his opponents at Halle, soon became the generally accepted way to refer to this brand of rationalistic Christianity.

NOTES TO THE SECOND LETTER

[1]The *CG* is divided into two main parts, the first dealing with "The Development of that Religious Self-Consciousness which is always both presupposed by and contained in every Christian Religious Affection" and the second presenting an "Explication of the Facts of the Religious Self-Consciousness, as they are determined by the Antithesis of Sin and Grace." Since both refer to elements that make up the Christian religious self-consciousness, they deserve to be included in a Christian dogmatics. Pt. 1 presupposes that self-consciousness, but it abstracts from the specific content of particular Christian experiences (*CG*, [2]§32,1). Therefore, Schleiermacher admits that this part will contain doctrines that will most easily coincide in expression with those of other faiths and which, omitting the distinction between theological and aesthetic faiths, may express only monotheism in general (*CG*, [2]§29,2). Yet the section is not a "universal or so-called natural theology" because the propositions arise from the religious self-consciousness itself and occur in the religious self-consciousness of the Christian, as particularized by the antithesis of sin and grace. In fact, the arrangement of the material in this part reflects a "distinctively Christian reference."

It would be possible to reverse the two parts, beginning with a discussion of the religious self-consciousness as determined by the antithesis of sin and grace and following with the explication of the religious self-consciousness presupposed by the contained in the Christian life. The reversal would necessitate a re-organization of the topics treated in each part, but it would not change the content of the work.

[2]Reference is to the Heidelberg Catechism of 1563, a chief doctrinal standard of the German Reformed Church. The Catechism is divided into three parts: pt. 1, Of Man's Misery; pt. 2, Of Man's Redemption; and pt. 3, Of Thankfulness. See Philip Schaff, ed., *The Creeds of Christendom, with a History and Critical Notes*, 3 vols. (New York: Harper & Row, 1877; reprint of the 4th ed., rev., Grand Rapids, Mich.: Baker Book House, 1966), 3:307-55.

An ordained minister of the Reformed Church, Schleiermacher endorsed and actively supported the union of Lutheran and Reformed Churches initiated by the Prussian monarch Friedrich Wilhelm III in 1817. Schleiermacher indicates that he wrote his dogmatics in light of that union (*CG*, [2]Vorrede, p. 4; *CF*, Pref., p. viii).

[3]Due in part to his philological training, Schleiermacher emphasized the need to be aware of the differences among literary genres. Since the key to his hermeneutical theory was the "circle" that each part must be understood in terms of the whole and each whole in terms of its parts, it is necessary to consider how elements are brought together into distinct "wholes" in catechisms and dogmatic theologies. In the *CG*, [1]§1,2; [2]§14,4, it is noted that catechisms and other popular expositions of doctrine designed for general church instruction do not belong within the field of dogmatics because they make no claim to erudition, systematic arrangement, and connection.

[4]E.g., *CG*, [1]§39; [2]§32,1.

[5]See above, pp. 40-43, 69-70, 76-78.

[6]See above, pp. 47-51.

[7]Nitzsch, "Rec. Delbrück's *Erörterungen*," p. 157, and n. I,
77 above.

[8]*CG*, 1§33; 2§29, esp. sect. 2.

[9]Ibid.

[10]Delbrück, *Erörterungen*, pp. 90ff. In 1826-27 two rounds of
letters passed between Delbrück and Schleiermacher about these
matters (see *ASL*, 4:366-83), but in the end the two can agree only
to disagree. See also nn. I, 6 and 92.

[11]*Collegium pietatis* refers to a group of church persons who
meet together for Bible study, devotions and fellowship. The formation of such groups was part of the pietistic program for church
reform during the eighteenth and nineteenth centuries.

[12]See e.g., *CG*, 1§§2-3 and §§34-35; 2§§15-16 and §§30-31.

[13]The reference is to the work of Denis Diderot (1713-84) and
the circle of *philosophes* who produced the *Encyclopédie*. Designed
to provide a convenient summary of human knowledge, popularizing
the scientific, social, cultural and moral themes of the Enlightenment, the *Encyclopédie* extended to thirty-five volumes (1751-80).
Articles on religion were phrased to cause as little offense as
possible for fear of censorship, but the advocacy of natural
religion and rationalistic faith was nonetheless evident. Six
editions of the immensely popular and controversial work appeared
in rapid succession, and its influence spread far beyond the bor-
ders of France.

[14]*CG*, 1§25,3; 2§22,2. In the second edition, Schleiermacher
alters the wording but not the substance of his point. Since the
Ebionites or Nazarenes were the first to regard Jesus as an ordinary man, the name "ebionitic" may be given to the heresy that
leaves no room ". . . for a distinctive superiority as a constitu-
ent of His [Jesus's] being, which must then be conceived under the
same form as that of all other men." This view entails that
". . . there must ultimately be posited in him also a need for
redemption, however absolutely small, and the fundamental relationship [between the redeemer and those who are to be redeemed]
is likewise essentially annulled."

[15]Steudel, "Die Frage," Stück 1, pp. 150-51, Steudel attempts
to show that study of the Old Testament cannot demonstrate messianic
prophecy in the sense of "a supernatural, direct effect of God,"
but it can provide references to the person or the work of the
Messiah which, corresponding to future events, could not have been
reached by the powers of the human spirit apart from divine
assistance given for this purpose.

[16]Karl Heinrich Sack, *Christliche Apologetik: Versuch eines
Handbuches* (Hamburg: F. Perthes, 1829), pp. 205-309. Although
Schleiermacher cited Sack's work (*CG*, 2§2), he expresses in this
letter to Lücke his doubt that Sack's appeal to Old Testament
prophecy and types as witnesses to Christian revelation in Jesus
Christ will withstand criticism and serve the purpose for which it
is intended.
     Biographical Note: The son of Friedrich S. C. Sack,
Reformed Bishop in Berlin who aided Schleiermacher in his youth,
Karl Heinrich (1789-1875) studied first at Göttingen and then
Berlin, where he came under Schleiermacher's influence. Following
a lectureship at Berlin in 1817, he was appointed pastor and

theological professor at Bonn. From 1847 to 1860 he was a member
of the Magdeburg Consistory.
    A friend of Lücke and Nitzsch, Sack is to be included among
those who sought to develop a mediating theology that built upon
Schleiermacher's work. In 1827 he joined these two in a defense
of Schleiermacher, *Über des Ansehen*, against Delbrück's criticism.
    Sack's major works, *Christliche Apologetik* and *Christliche
Polemik* (Hamburg: F. Perthes, 1838), were influenced by Schleiermacher's *Brief Outline*, but in crucial respects they deviated from
that position. Unlike his teacher, Sack attempts to provide
philosophical and biblical evidences for the truth of Christianity,
with the result that apologetics is to supply the foundation of
Christianity as a divine fact and polemics is to defend church
and faith against dangerous errors.

    [17]See the discussions of Judaism in the *CG*, [1]§§15-16, 22;
[2]§§8-9, 12, and [1]§18,1; [2]§11,4, where Schleiermacher treats the
differing ways in which Moses and Christ can be said to be the
"founders" of Judaism and Christianity, respectively.

    [18]Sack, *Christliche Apologetik*, p. 447.

    [19]Bretschneider published a study on the Johannine literature
in 1820, *Probabilia de evangelii et epistolarum Joannis apostoli
indole et origine* (Leipzig: Johann Ambrosius Barth, 1820).
Writing in Latin in order to avoid offending non-scholars, Bretschneider argued that historical-critical research proved it un-
likely that the author of the Fourth Gospel had been an eyewitness
or an apostle. His argument was rejected by most scholars, and
after four years of controversy, Bretschneider himself seemed to
doubt his conclusions, explaining that he had written the book
only so that the issue might be debated and that his theory, if
in error, might be refuted. A brief but helpful discussion is
available in Werner Georg Kümmel, *The New Testament: The History
of the Investigation of Its Problems*, trans. S. MacLean Gilmour
and Howard Clark Kee (Nashville and New York: Abingdon Press, 1972),
pp. 85-86 and 420.

    [20]David Schulz, *Die christliche Lehre vom heiligen Abendmahl*
(Leipzig: Johann Ambrosius Barth, 1824), pp. 302ff. Schulz considers Matthew to be the last of the synoptic gospels to be written
and discounts its historical reliability on that basis.
    Biographical Note: Schulz (1779-1854) was trained at Halle
and Leipzig and taught at Halle, Frankfurt, and Breslau. In
1819 he became a member of the Consistory of Silesia. An outspoken
advocate of rationalist theology, his arguments with conservatives
led to his dismissal from the Consistory in 1845. In addition to
the work cited by Schleiermacher, his major works included
Der Brief an die Hebräer (Leipzig: Johann Ambrosius Barth, 1818);
Die christliche Lehre vom Glauben (Leipzig: Johann Ambrosius Barth,
1824); and *Das Wesen und Treiben der Berliner Evangelische
Kirchenzeitung beleuchtet*, 2 vols. in 1 (Breslau: Ferdinand Hirt,
1839-40), which was a polemic against that conservative party or-
gan. Hengstenberg's attack against rationalism at Halle led
Schulz to join Daniel Georg von Cölln to write in defense of aca-
demic freedom *(Über theologische Lehrfreiheit auf den evangelischen
Universitäten und deren Beschränkung durch symbolische Bücher*
[Breslau: Goschorsky, 1830]). That debate in turn prompted
Schleiermacher to take up the issue. See Friedrich Schleiermacher,
Kleine Schriften und Predigten, ed. Hayo Gerders and Emanuel Hirsch,
vol. 2: *Schriften zur Kirchen-und Bekenntnisfrage*, ed. Hayo Gerders
(Berlin: Walter de Gruyter & Co., 1969), pp. 225-78.

[21]See the discussion of the authority and inspiration of scripture in *CG*, [1]§21,2-3; [2]§14, Postscript. Cf. Schleiermacher, *Hermeneutics: The Handwritten Manuscripts*, ed. Heinz Kimmerle, trans. James Duke and Jack Forstman, (Missoula, MT: American Academy of Religion/Scholars Press, 1977), pp. 45, 87, 104-8, 143-44, and 216.

[22]The conflict between rationalism and supernaturalism periodically prompted calls for the suppression or expulsion of the rationalists. Here Schleiermacher may refer to the Leipzig Disputation of 1825, at which the faculty issued a statement dismissing the rationalists from the church. Although that pronouncement was later amended to state that the rationalists should, for the sake of their own consciences, leave the church voluntarily, it created a storm of controversy.

[23]Debates over the "Fundamental Articles" of Christianity were introduced into seventeenth century protestant orthodoxy by the Lutheran, Nikolaus Hunnius (1563-1643), who served as Professor of Theology at Wittenberg and then as a pastor and superintendent in Lübeck. In his works, *Epitome Credendorum* (1625) and *Theologicae de Fundamentali Dissensu Doctrinae Evangelicae--Lutheranae et Calvinianae seu Reformate* (1628), Hunnius sought to distinguish between those articles of faith which constitute or support the foundation of faith itself, and so must be known and affirmed by every Christian, and those articles which are true statements of faith, but need not be known or affirmed in order to gain salvation. In the works of later Protestant theologians the distinction underwent numerous permutations.

[24]Cf. *CG*, [1]§18 and [2]§11, esp. sect. 4, where the material has been reorganized and rewritten, but the basic position remains the same. Among the changes are a change in tone, as Schleiermacher drops the charge that those who consider Jesus Christ as the founder of Christianity in the same way that Moses and Mohammed founded Judaism and Islam are also those who deny the distinctiveness of Christianity.
He adds: "Not that we mean here to exclude at the outset from the Christian communion all those who differ from this presentation of the matter . . . in holding that Christ was only later endowed with redeeming power, provided only that this power is recognized as something different from the mere communication of doctrine and a rule of life" ([2]§11,4).

[25]Question Fifteen of the Heidelberg Catechism asks, "What manner of mediator, then, must we seek?" The answer is, "One who is a true and sinless man, and yet more powerful than all creatures, that is, one who is at the same time true God." This statement is followed by Question Sixteen, "Why must he be a true and sinless man?" and Question Seventeen, "Why must he be at the same time true God?" (Schaff, *Creeds of Christendom*, 3:312).

[26]Schleiermacher refers to the epitaph on the grave of King Midas, cited in Plato's *Phaedrus*, 264 D (cf. Delbrück, *Der verewigte Schleiermacher*, p. 96), which is rendered in German:

Hier an den Midas Grab erblickst du mich eherne Jüngfrau
Bis nicht Wasser mehr fliesst, noch erblühn hockstämmige
    Bäume.
Muss ich verweilen allhier an dem viel beträneten Denkmal,
Dass auch der Wanderer wisse, wo Midal liege begraben.

In *Works of Plato*, 4 vols. in 1 (New York: Dial Press, n.d.), pp. 248-29, Benjamin Jowett's quite free translation of the Greek reads:

I am a Maiden of brass
I lie on the tomb of Midas
While waters flow and tall trees grow
Here am I.

On Midas' tearful tomb I lie
I am to tell the passers by
That Midas sleeps in earth below.

[27]Tzschirner, *Briefe eines Deutschen,* p. 29.

[28]Ibid., pp. 26ff. Schelling concluded his *System der trans-
zendentalen Idealismus* (1802) with the reconciliation of the finite
and the Infinite through art. E.T.: *System of Transcendental
Idealism,* trans. Peter Heath (Charlottesville, Va.: University
Press of Virginia, 1978). Francis August René, Viscount de
Chateaubriand (1768-1848), was a romantic author, monarchist and
statesman. In his *Génie du christianisme, ou beautés de la
religion chrétienne* of 1802 (E.T.: *The Genius of Christianity; or
the Spirit and Beauty of the Christian Religion,* trans. Charles
I. White, 2d, rev. ed. [Baltimore, Md.: John Murray & Co., 1856;
reprint ed.: New York: Howard Fertig, 1976]), Chateaubriand defended Christianity and the Roman Catholic Church against the
destructive criticisms of the *philosophes* by appealing to feeling
rather than to reason. He argued that Christianity is validated
by the art and civilization it has produced and by its contribu-
tions to the intellectual and spiritual ideals of humanity. See
also n. I, 79 above.

[29]Schleiermacher discusses the three forms of dogmatic propositions in relation to Christian faith itself and to the task of
theology in the *CG,* [1]§§34-35; [2]§§30-31. The first form, descriptions of human states of mind, is primary, whereas the other two,
conceptions of divine attributes and statements about the constitution of the world, are to be accepted and elaborated only inasmuch
as they can be developed from the primary form.

[30]Baur, *Comparatur,* pp. 7-13.

[31]*CG,* [1]§34,3; [2]§30,3. The word "system" is used for *Lehrge-
bäude,* which was present in the first edition but omitted in the
second. (But see [2]§20,2, where it appears.)

Although it cannot be denied that, strictly speaking,
the first form suffices for completing the analysis of
Christian piety and it would be best to elaborate this
form exclusively, since only by means of it could
the others be grasped in their true dogmatic meaning,
yet the other forms cannot be excluded from a Christian
system without causing it to lose its historical position and its ecclesiastical character.

[32]The difference between true dogmatics and a system that sets
forth the private convictions of Christians is discussed in *CG,*
[1]§1,1 and §29,3; 2§19,3 and §25,1. The term "historical position"
is explained in *CG,* [1]§34,3; [2]§30,2.

[33]*CG,* [1]§34 states that "these three forms have always existed
next to each other in dogmatics," and [1]§34,2 reads: "that every
Christian doctrine of faith [*Glaubenslehre*] has always contained
propositions of all three forms needs no proof."

[34]Baur, *Comparatur*, p. 9. This work was published as the
Tübinger akademisches Osterprogramm.

[35]The distinction between the "old Tübingen school" of biblical
supernaturalism (e.g., Gottlob Christian Storr, Johann Friedrich
Flatt, and Friedrich Süskind) and the "Tübingen school" associated
with Baur had not yet emerged. In 1826 a reorganization of the
faculty brought Baur and others to the school. Steudel, who had
taught there since 1805, survived the changes, and, although he
represented the older tradition, he worked well personally with
his younger colleagues.

[36]Johann Friedrich Röhr, "Besprechung Schleiermachers *Glaubenslehre*," *Kritischer Prediger-Bibliothek* 4 (1823): 383.
   Biographical Note: Röhr (1777-1848) studied at Leipzig,
where he came under the influence of Kantian critical philosophy.
He became a popularizer of rationalistic Christianity through his
work as pastor in several churches and as Chief Court Preacher and
General Superintendent (after 1820) at Weimar, as well as through
such publications as his *Briefe über den Rationalismus* (Aachen:
J. Frosch, 1813) and the *Grund- und Glaubenssätze der evangelisch-
protestantischen Kirche* (Neustadt a.d. Orla: J. K. G. Wagner, 1832),
and through his editorship of several journals for pastors, including the *Kritischer Prediger-Bibliothek* (1820-48). Along with
Karl Bretschneider in Gotha and J. Schuderoff in Ronneburg, he
helped make Thuringia a stronghold for the rationalist party within the church.
   In a letter to J. C. Gass dated December 20, 1823, Schleiermacher explains that the publisher Heinrichshofen persuaded him to
accept joint editorial responsibilities with Röhr and Schuderoff
for the *Magazin von Fest-, Gelegensheit- und anderen Predigten und
kleineren Amtsreden* (1823-29). Thirty-six of Schleiermacher's
sermons, along with several shorter essays, were published in
that journal. Schleiermacher also states that "my colleague
Röhr has expressed himself about my dogmatics in his *Prediger
Zeitung*, but I have learned nothing from his criticisms" (*ASL*, 4:
316-21).

[37]*CG*, [1]§31; [2]§28, deals with the "dialectical character" of
language. In a note to [1]§31, Schleiermacher states that "dialectical is here taken in its purely ancient sense in which it means
that which is artistically proper in speech inasmuch as the speech
is directed to expressing and communicating knowledge." He then
explains that this view implies that in dogmatics there can be no
philosophical proofs or reference to speculative principles (*CG*,
[1]§31,1; cf. [2]§28,1). In [2]§28,2 (cf. [1]§31,2) the term is used
again:

> If, however, Dogmatics is to fulfil its proper voca-
> tion, i.e., both to clear up the misconceptions which
> ever and again tend to arise in the whole business of
> making communications from the immediate religious life
> of the Christian, and also, so far as in it lies, to
> prevent such misconceptions by the norm it has estab-
> lished, not only is a dialectically formed vocabulary
> indispensable in the establishing of its system of
> doctrine, but also as strict and systematic an arrange-
> ment of the subject-matter as possible.

[38]Schleiermacher refers to his *Brief Outline*, which defines
the nature of and the interrelations among the theological disci-
plines. These formal definitions are crucial for understanding
the Introduction to the *Glaubenslehre*, but they are not to determine the actual content of the dogmatics itself.

[39]Lücke, *Kommentar über die Schriften des Evangelisten Johannes.*

[40]Delbrück, *Erörterungen,* p. 94.

[41]Ibid., p. 140, where Delbrück asserts that the church teacher must maintain that sinfulness is universal, thus positing that the human will is weak, and must also acknowledge human freedom and responsibility.

[42]Baur, *Comparatur,* pp. 3-6, 14.

[43]The discussion in this paragraph and the following one is in response to Baur, "Anzeige," p. 242.

[44]Schleiermacher, *On Religion,* especially Speech Five, "The Religions," pp. 272-322.

[45]Redemption was treated especially in the *CG,* [1]§§18-22. The materials were reorganized ([2]§§11-14) under the heading "Presentations of Christianity in Its Peculiar Essence: Propositions Borrowed from Apologetics." In [1]§18,3 redemption is said to mean "a constraint [*Hemmung*] of life lifted and a better condition produced." [2]§11,2 reads: "the term itself is in this realm merely figurative, and signifies in general a passage from an evil condition, which is represented as a state of captivity or constraint, into a better condition--this is the passive side of it. But it also signifies the help given in that process by some other person, and this is the active side of it."

[46]Baur, "Anzeige," pp. 247ff.

[47]Friedrich Heinrich Christian Schwarz, "Rec. Schleiermacher's *Glaubenslehre,*" *Heidelburger Jahrbücher der Literatur* 15 (1822), nos. 54, 60-62, and 16 (1823), nos. 14-15 and 21-22.
    Biographical Note: Schwarz (1766-1827) was born in Giessen and studied at the University there. He served in various pastorates before his call to Heidelberg in 1804 as Professor of Theology and Pedagogy. His dogmatics, *Grundriss der kirchlichen-protestantischen Dogmatik* (Heidelberg: Winter, 1816), was written in light of a union between the Lutheran and Reformed churches, and on behalf of himself and other (unnamed) authors who wrote theology with union in mind, Schwarz contested Schleiermacher's claim to be the first to have written for the united church ("Rec. Schleiermacher's *Glaubenslehre,*" No. 54, p. 855; cf. Schleiermacher, *CG,* [1]Vorrede, p. viii; [2]Vorrede, p. 4 where credit is given to "G. K. R. Schwarz"). Schwarz's fame, however, was due chiefly to his teaching and research in educational theory and practice, as set forth in his *Lehrbuch der Pädagogik und Didaktik* (Heidelberg: Mohr, 1805) and other works.

[48]Schwarz, "Rec. Schleiermacher's *Glaubenslehre,*" 15 (1822): 959ff., esp. 966. *CG,* [1]§6 states: "In order to ascertain what the essence of Christian piety consists of, we must go beyond Christianity and take our standpoint over it in order to compare it with other types of faith." Cf. *CG,* [2]§2.

[49]*CG,* [1]§§14-17 are revised as [2]§§7-10 and grouped together under the title "The Diversities of Religious Communions in General: Propositions Borrowed From the Philosophy of Religion." Also added is a postscript to [2]§7,2-3, which states, "By Philosophy of Religion is understood a critical presentation of the differing existing forms of religious communion, as constituting,

when taken collectively, the complete phenomenon of piety in human
nature." See also Schleiermacher, *Brief Outline*, §§6, 23, and 43.

[50]Sack, *Christliche Apologetik*, p. 75. Cf. *CG*, 1§19-20 and
2§§10-11, which are designated as propositions borrowed from apologetics. Sack's response to the *The Letters to Lücke* illumine the
issue (*Christliche Apologetik*, 2d ed., p. 123, n. 1). Here Sack
reiterates that Schleiermacher's belief that the absolute, true
revelation was in Christ may be properly called "historical,"
because Schleiermacher uses the word revelation, in a strict
sense, only for that which is derived from the person of Christ.
Sack claims to understand that Schleiermacher wishes "historical" revelation to provide the basis for his entire dogmatics, and
he stresses that he too used the word in its dogmatic sense. Since
Schleiermacher will not use the term revelation in connection with
the concept religion per se or in reference to non-Christian religions, Sack concedes that it would have been better to say that
Schleiermacher does not consider the concept serviceable [*haltbar*]
for apologetic purposes. The issue, then, arises at this point:

> Now when Schleiermacher says of me that I "call the
> historical dogmatic and the dogmatic history," then
> this at first glance has the appearance of being a
> confusion rightly attributed to me. Yet the confu-
> sion appears nowhere in my work. The opposition
> between him and me is not in the different names
> given to the areas [dogmatics and apologetics]
> but in the claim that the concept [of revelation]
> is apologetically-theologically serviceable as that
> of a fact even apart from the person of Christ--a
> statement that I affirm and Schleiermacher denies.

[51]In *CG*, 1§1, Schleiermacher states: "Dogmatic theology is
the science which systemizes the doctrine prevalent in a Christian
Church at a particular time." This definition--except that the
word "given" replaces "particular"--is shifted to §19 in the 2d
ed. Cf. Schleiermacher, *Brief Outline*, §97: "The systematic representation of doctrine which is current at any given time, whether
for the Church in general, when division does not prevail, or for
any particular party within the Church, we designate by the term
'dogmatics' or 'dogmatic theology,'"

[52]Schleiermacher, *Brief Outline*, especially §§5-9 and 213-16.

[53]In a review in *FThPh* 1 (1828): 148, Jakob Friedrich Fries
agrees with Schleiermacher that religion has its sources in feeling rather than in thinking or morality, but he argues that any
account of religion which claims to be true is by its very nature
based in some sort of philosophizing. Unless religious persons
have thought out their philosophical position, they will inevitably think in the philosophical terms common to their day.
    Biographical Note: Jakob Friedrich Fries (1773-1842) was a
philosopher whose interests ranged from metaphysics, ethics, and
religion to mathematics, physics, and psychology. Like Schleiermacher he had been trained at schools of the Moravian Brethern at
Niesky and Barby. Later studies at Leipzig and Jena led him away
from Moravian pietism to Kantianism, but the influence of this
background is evidenced by his conviction that feeling is the point
of contact between the Infinite and the finite. Fries taught at
Jena (1805), Heidelberg (1805-1816), and again at Jena (1816-43),
although during this second tenure he was for a time (1818-24)
suspended for his "liberal" political persuasions.
    Fries sought to build upon and correct Kant's thought by em-
phasizing the descriptive-empirical, psychological, or

anthropological--character of critical philosophy. His opposition
to post-Kantian speculative idealism was made known in his thesis
Reinhold, Fichte and Schelling (Leipzig: A. L. Reinecke, 1803).
His first major work on religion was *Wissen, Glauben und Ahnung*
(Jena: Gopfert, 1805). Influenced by Schleiermacher's *On Religion*,
Fries argued that the essence of religion was feeling, where a
presentiment [*Ahnung*] of the Infinite gives rise to images that
afford positive but not conceptual knowledge of God, freedom, and
immortality. Among his chief works are: *Neue Kritik der Vernunft*,
3 vols. (Heidelberg: Mohr und Zimmer, 1807); *System der Meta-
physik* (Heidelberg: C. F. Winter, 1824); and *Handbuch der psychis-
chen Anthropologie, oder der Lehre von der Natur des Menschlichen
Geistes*, 2 vols. in 1 (Jena: Cröker, 1820-21).

[54]In a response to Schleiermacher, Fries shows that this distinction between a doctrine of a particular religious community
and a doctrine arising from speculative theology does not function
in the same way for him as for Schleiermacher. If Schleiermacher
is merely describing someone else's religious faith, then Fries
agrees that philosophy does not enter in. But if Schleiermacher
is speaking as a theologian who sets forth the truth claims of
the religious community of which he is a part, then he also speaks
as one who justifies, or criticizes, elements of church doctrine
on the basis of his own philosophical viewpoint ("Über Schleiermacher's zweites Sendschreiben über seine *Glaubenslehre*," *FThPh*
2 (1828): 138-39. According to Fries, it is clear that Schleiermacher's system contains a critique of the doctrine of religion
of the evangelical church which is based on the principles of the
author's own philosophy, especially the "philosophical" view that
the human feeling of utter dependency is basic to all religious
conviction.

[55]*CG*, 1§31,4: "The expressions which occur in the *Glaubenslehre*,
indeed form, insofar as they refer back to the pious feeling, a
distinct [*eigenes*] area of language, namely the didactically
religious. . . ." See also *CG*, 2§28,1. Fries counters the argument made in *The Letters to Lücke* with the following remark:

>With what Schleiermacher says about the levels of
>language in matters of religion between the com-
>pletely popular [*volksmässigen*] and the dogmatic,
>I am completely in agreement. I relate the
>dilemma attributed to me not to language but to
>one's self-conception. The dogmatician either
>tells only about the opinions of others or he
>expresses him own convictions. The latter now,
>I maintain, cannot occur without philosophical
>self-reflection, and a dogmatician who has not
>tried to work out his philosophical view will
>think in the philosophy which in the historical
>development of religious language has become
>common for his day ("Über Schleiermacher's
>zweites Sendschreiben," p. 139).

[56]Pt. 1 of Kant's *Religion within the Limits of Reason Alone*,
pp. 15-39, deals with the radical evil within human nature.
Radical evil refers to the human propensity to subordinate the
incentive of the moral law to that of the law of self love,

>. . . and since this very propensity must in the end
>be sought in a will which is free, and can therefore
>be imputed, it is morally evil. This evil is
>radical, because it corrupts the ground of all
>maxims; it is moreover, as a natural propensity,

inextirpable by human powers, since extirpation
could occur only through good maxims, and cannot
take place when the subjective ground of all
maxims is postulated as corrupt; yet at the
same time it must be possible to overcome it,
since it is found in man, a being whose actions
are free (pp. 31-32).

[57]See n. I, 99 above.

[58]One might think here of Anthony Ashley Cooper, third Earl
of Shaftesbury (1671-1713), who related moral values to the
"aesthetic sense" or faculty, and Francis Hutcheson (1654-1746),
who found the moral sense to be rooted in inward affections and
dispositions. See Richard B. Brandt, *The Philosophy of Schleiermacher* (New York: Harper and Brothers, 1941), pp. 179-80, note.

[59]Steudel, "Die Frage," Stück 1, pp. 94-95, where it is said
that Schleiermacher and Schott are alike in seeking to reconcile
opposing positions (rationalism and supernaturalism) at the very
point that they are irreconcilable. In *Brief über Religion und
christlichen Offenbarungsglauben als Worte des Friedens as
streitende Parteien* (Jena: Crökerschen Buchhandlung, 1826),
Schott expresses appreciation for Schleiermacher's attempt to reconcile rationalism and supernaturalism by means of a mediating
theology. Schott hopes to build and improve upon Schleiermacher's
effort.
    Biographical Note: August Friedrich Schott (1780-1835)
taught at the Universities of Leipzig, Wittenberg, and Jena during
the course of his academic career. As Professor of Homiletics and
founder of the Homiletics Seminar at Jena, he was best known for
his publications in that area, especially *Die Theorie der Beredsamkeit, mit besonderer Anwendung auf die christliche Beredsamkeit,
in ihrem ganzen Umfänge dargestellt,* 3 pts. (Leipzig: Johann
Ambrosius Barth, 1815-28).

[60]Ibid., p. 134. Steudel claims that the opposition between
rationalism and supernaturalism cannot be overcome because the
entire issue comes down to a question that can be answered only by
a "yes" or a "no."

> Do you recognize outside of that which is given in
> humanity lying in itself and developed from itself,
> also a historically presented, credible [*glaubwürdige*]
> source of instruction about divine things, such that
> the content of this instruction must be accepted as
> true--not because it belongs among those truths of
> human reason discoverable by man himself, but be-
> cause it is confirmed [*beglaubigt*] by God as the
> object of religious satisfaction [*Glaubensbefried-
> egende*]?

This the rationalists must deny and the supernaturalists affirm.

[61]Ibid., pp. 109-12. Cf. *CG*, 2§43,3. Schleiermacher had claimed
that Jesus and the apostles believed in and spoke about angels not
out of any firm conviction about their existence and their religious significance but out of a conviction in a broad sense, that
is, as a popular idea shared by everyone in the day. Like every
human being, Christ accepted such popular ideas. But since they
did not arise from his religious consciousness and so did not
have a definite religious intent, these ideas are not binding on
Christians.

Steudel, however, counters with his formulation of the supernaturalist view. Jesus Christ was a person not only with a divine life but with a knowledge of truth that was neither contaminated nor contaminable by the unfounded ideas of his age. Any doubts one might have about the existence of such spiritual beings may be put to rest because the statements of Jesus Christ provide sufficient testimony for belief.

[62]Ibid., pp. 110-11. Steudel correctly notes that Schleiermacher's explanation of why Jesus spoke of angels differs from the usual theory of accomodation, which proposed that Jesus made use of such popular notions in order to communicate with his contemporaries even though he himself knew that the ideas were not true. Much in Steudel's response is ironic or even satirical. He contends that, given Schleiermacher's view, it must be assumed that the activity of the archetypal Christ in humans today leads them beyond the archetypal Christ himself, asmuch as they can now distinguish between what was a firm conviction with a definite reference and what was merely a general conviction adopted from the culture of the day. "And how fortunate it is," Steudel concludes, "that our age can congratulate itself on having been given the enlightenment [to tell] what in that which has come from God belongs to conviction in the strict sense and what belongs to conviction in the broad sense" (p. 111).

[63]Although Roman Catholics had gained some measure of religious freedom, they were denied seats in Parliament, even to represent Ireland, which was of course overwhelmingly Roman Catholic. The reference here is to the debate that arose over the Emancipation Act of 1829, which allowed Roman Catholics--with the exception of the clergy--to participate more fully in electoral and parliamentary processes.

[64]Rust, *De nonnullis*, 56, 61, and 65. See n. I, 17 above.

[65]Friedrich Wähner, "Reç. Schleiermacher's Glaubenslehre," *Hermes* 22 (1824): 275-344 and 23 (1824): 214-74.

[66]On Nitzsch, see n. I, 22 above.

[67]August Detlev Christian Twesten, *Vorlesungen über die Dogmatik der evangelischen-lutheranischen Kirche*. Vol. 1 appeared in 1826 (Hamburg: F. Parthes), but pt. 1 of vol. 2 was not issued until 1837, three years after Schleiermacher's death.
  Biographical Note: Twesten (1789-1876), a student of Schleiermacher's, was Professor of Philosophy and Theology at Kiel from 1814 and became in 1835 Schleiermacher's successor at Berlin. In addition to his teaching, he served on the Consistory and, after 1852, on the Church Council (*Oberkirchenrates*). His major publications, in addition to his dogmatics, were *Die Logik, insbesondere die Analytik* (Schleswig: Königl. Taubstummen-Institut, 1825) and a study of Schleiermacher's ethics: *Schleiermacher's Grundriss der philosophischen Ethik* (Berlin: G. Reimer, 1841).

[68]Schleiermacher, *On Religion*, chap. 1 and n. 2 on p. 63, which was added for the second edition.

[69]"I fear the Greeks even when they bear gifts."

[70]Baur, Bretschneider and Tzschirner link Schleiermacher with Schelling (see n. I, 14 above). Rust, however, identifies a dependence of Schleiermacher on Jacobi (see n. I, 15 above). The irony in these divergent interpretations is heightened when

one considers that much of Jacobi's fame was due to his polemics
against speculative idealism, which he believed to have revived
Spinoza's pantheism.

[71]Delbrück, *Erörterungen*, p. 41.

[72]Steudel, "Die Frage," Stück 1, p. 51.   Stück 2 (1828), pp.
74-199, was not available to Schleiermacher.

[73]The reference here is to Baur's term "ideal rationalism"
(see n. I, 12 above).   Knapp refers to Schleiermacher as a poetic
or sentimental rationalist, and Schott calls him a rational
supernaturalist.

[74]Schleiermacher began teaching at Halle in the winter semester
of 1804-5.

TABLE OF COMPARATIVE PAGINATION

The beginning of each translated page of *On the Glaubenslehre* may be correlated to the pagination of the Mulert edition as follows:

The First Letter		The Second Letter	
Translation	Mulert	Translation	Mulert
33	7	55	30
34	8	56	31
35	9	57	32
36	10	58	33
37	11	59	34
38	13	60	35
39	14	61	36
40	15	62	37
41	16	63	38
42	17	64	39
43	18	65	40
44	19	66	42
45	20	67	43
46	21	68	44
47	22	69	45
48	23	70	46
49	24	71	48
50	26	72	49
51	27	73	50
52	28	74	51
53	29	75	52
		76	53
		77	55
		78	56
		79	57
		80	58
		81	59
		82	60
		83	61
		84	62
		85	63
		86	64
		87	65
		88	67
		89	67

INDEX OF NAMES IN THE TEXT OF THE LETTERS

Baur, F. C.,   36-37, 71-72, 76-77,
                                   83

Braniss, C. F.,   46

Bretschneider, K. G.,   38, 40,
                           44-45, 48

Chateaubriand, Francois René de,70

Delbrück, J. Fr. F.,   36, 49-50,
                           67, 75-76

Fichte, J. G.,   82

Fries, J. Fr.,   80-82

Hase, Karl,   48

Jacobi, Fr. H.,   36, 87

John,   62

Kant, Immanuel,   82

Klaiber, C. B.,   37

Leibnitz, G. W.,   52, 82

Luther, Martin,   40-41

Marheinecke, P. K.,   48

Nitzsch, K. I.,   47, 52, 85

Paul,   62

Plato,   84

Röhr, J. F.,   72

Rust, Isaaco,   36

Sack, K. H.,   65-66, 78-79

Schelling, J. Fr. W. von,   36, 48,
                               70, 87

Schulz, David,   66-67

Schwarz, F. H. C.,   77-78

Socrates,   84

Spinoza, Benedict, 48-49,
                          51

Steudel, J. C. F.,   37,
              44, 65, 83-84, 88

Twesten, A. D.,   87

Tzschirner, H. G.,   39,
                  41, 48, 70

Wolff, Christian, 52, 82

INDEX OF NAMES IN THE NOTES TO THE LETTERS

An (*) designates where a biographical sketch is to be found.

Ammon, C. Fr. von.   107*

Anselm,   111

Aristippus,   101

Aristotle,   112

Augustine,   113

Baur, F. C.,   95, 98*-100, 102,
                        104, 112-14,
                   123-25, 129-30

Böhme, C. F.,   114*

Braniss, C. F.,   96*, 112-13

Bretschneider, K. G.,   97*-102,
                   105, 110-12, 114,
                   121, 124, 129-30

Cassian, John,   105

Chateaubriand, Francois René de,
                   96-97, 123

Cölln, D. G. von,   121

Daub, Carl,   97

Delbrück, J. Fr. F.,   95-96*, 101,
                   113, 116-18, 120,
                   122-23, 125, 130

de Wette, W. M. L.,   95

Diderot, Denis,   120

Fichte, J. G.,   100

Flatt, J. F.,   124

Friedrich II (the Great),   118

Friedrich Wilhelm III,   119

Fries, J. F.,   113, 126*-27

Gass, J. C.,   96, 114, 116,
                   124

Gieseler, J. K. L.,   95

Goethe, J. W. von,   114, 116

Harms, Klaus,   109

Hase, Karl,   100

Hegel, G. Fr. W.,   97-98

Hengstenberg, E. W.,   121

Hunnius, N.,   122

Hutcheson, Francis,   128

Jacobi, Fr. J.,100*, 114, 129

Kant, Immanuel,   100, 102,
                   106, 126-28

Klaiber, C. B.,   101*-3,
                   109, 114-15

Knapp, Albert,   103*, 113

Leibnitz, G. W.,   118

Lessing, G. E., 100, 102, 114

Lücke, G. Fr. L.,   95*-96,
                   114, 116, 120, 125

Marheinecke, P. K.,   97, 100,
                        108

Mendelssohn, Moses,   100

Neander, J. A. W.,   95

Nitzsch, K. I.,   95-96, 99,
                   102*, 112-13, 116,
                   118, 120-21, 129

Paulus, H. E. G.,   97

Planck, G. F.,   95

Plato, Platonists, 108, 113, 122-23

Pythagoreans,   113

Rätze, J. G.,   108-9*

Reinhard, F. V.,   102, 107

Röhr, J. F.,   124*

Rust, Isaaco,   97*, 15, 17, 19-20,
                              49, 129

Sack, F. S. C.,   120*-21

Sack, K. H.,   95-96, 104, 116,
                     120*-21,   126

Schelling, W. J. von, 99-100, 104,
                          114, 123

Schmid, H. J. T.,   99*, 107-8

Schlegel, Fr.,   116

Schott, A. F.,   110, 112-13

Schuderoff, Jonathan,   124

Schulz, David,   121

Schwarz, F. H. C.,   125

Semler, J. S.,   106

Shaftesbury, (A. A. Cooper),   128

Spinoza, Benedict,   100, 113-16,
                          129-30

Steudel, J. C. Fr.,   104*, 109-110,
                   120, 124, 128-30

Stoics,   113

Storr, G. C.,   124

Strauss, D. Fr.,   95

Süskind, Friedrich,   124

Twesten, A. D. C.,   108,
                               129*

Tzschirner, H. G.,   96*-97,
                   99, 106-7, 114,
                       123, 129

Ullmann, Carl,   95

Umbreit, F. W. C.,   95

Wähner, Friedrich,   129

Wieland, C. M.,   100

Wolff, Christian,   118